THE LIBRARY OF TRADITIONAL WISDOM

The Library of Traditional Wisdom has as its aim to present a series of works founded on Tradition, this term being defined as the transmission, over time, of permanent and universal truths, whose written sources are the revealed Scriptures as well as the writings of great spiritual masters.

This series is thus dedicated to the *Sophia Perennis* or *Religio Perennis* which is the timeless metaphysical truth underlying the diverse religions, together with its essential methodological consequences.

It is in the light of the *Sophia Perennis*, which views every religion "from within," that may be found the keys of an adequate understanding which, joined to the sense of the sacred, alone can safeguard the irreplaceable values and genuine spiritual possibilities of the great religions.

Stations
of Wisdom

Frithjof Schuon

World Wisdom Books, Inc.

Contents

Published in French as
Les Stations de la Sagesse
Maisonneuve et Larose, Paris, 1992

Previous English editions
John Murray, London, 1961
Perennial Books, London, 1980

Library of Congress Cataloging-in-Publication Data

Schuon, Frithjof, 1907-
   [Les stations de la sagesse. English]
   Stations of Wisdom / by Frithjof Schuon. — A rev. translation from the French.
      p. cm.
   Includes bibliographical references and index.
   ISBN 0-941532-18-6 (pbk. : alk. paper) : $12.00
   1. Faith and reason. 2. Intellect—Religious aspects. 3. Faith. I. Title.
BL51.S46583   1995
291.2—dc20

The cover photo is one of the three great portals (*gopuram*)
at the temple of Chidambaram, India;
by permission of Erwin Böhm, photographer.

Printed on acid-free paper in The United States of America

For information address World Wisdom Books, Inc.
P. O. Box 2682, Bloomington, Indiana 47402-2682

Preface

It has often and justly been said that the ills of our times
come from the scission between faith and science; paradox-
ically enough, the beginnings of this scission are to be
found within faith itself, or at least in its extrinsic and
subjective aspect, in the sense that faith has not been, or is
not, adequately buttressed by commentaries of the sapiential order, or that in the minds of most people sentimental
rather than metaphysical reasons have been dominant; the
intellectual element, or need for causal explanations, thus
left neglected outside faith was bound in the end to turn
against it, though "from below" and on a purely rational,
material level. But the scission in question has yet other
causes, subjective as well as objective: on the one hand, the
"intellectual worldliness" inaugurated by the Renaissance
and by Descartes resulted in a weakening of contemplative
intelligence and religious instinct, and on the other hand,
new factors — inventions and discoveries of every kind —
were to profit from this weakening and have seemed to
constitute a glaring contradiction to the tenets of faith.
Modern man seems to be less and less capable of intellectual resistance to the suggestiveness of facts which, though
belonging to the natural order, lie outside the ordinary,
normal experience of human beings. To be able to combine the religious symbolism of Heaven with the astronomical fact of the stellar galaxies in a single consciousness, an
intelligence is needed which is more than just rational —

unless there be faith such as is not given to everyone; and this brings us to the crucial problem of intellection and, as a consequence, to that of gnosis and esoterism. All things considered, the hostility of the medieval Church towards the new astronomical theories is explained by this, and is justified a posteriori in view of the consequences.

But scepticism does not always need the help of Cartesian philosophy to implant itself, for the latter would be sterile without a soil ready to receive it; in fact, all "worldliness" is a breach through which, given favorable conditions, the spirit of doubt and of denial of the supernatural is made welcome. No people, however contemplative, can in the long run resist this psychological effect of modern science — the difference, in this respect, between men bearing the mark of the Renaissance and the traditional collectivities of Asia and elsewhere is only relative — and that clearly shows how "abnormal" this science is in relation to the basic facts of human nature. It is only too evident that while no knowledge is bad in itself and in principle, many forms of knowledge can be harmful in fact, just because they do not correspond to man's hereditary habits and are imposed on him without his being spiritually prepared; the soul finds it hard to accommodate facts that nature has not offered to its experience, unless it be enlightened with metaphysical knowledge or with an impregnable sanctity. That is why traditional doctrines, and above all the Revelations from which they derive, take full account of collective and normal human experience, which constitutes an indisputable basis since in fact we are men. These doctrines provide a comprehensive and qualitative knowledge of the cosmos, while at the same time conveying the idea that the cosmos is but nothing in comparison with the Absolute and that the Absolute in any case eludes the means of investigation of specifically human knowledge. The principle of "normal" and "providential" limitation of the data of experience applies moreover also to art: art has need of limits imposed by nature, at any rate insofar as it concerns a collectivity, which by definition is passive and "unconscious"; one has only to put the resources of machines and of the chemical industry at the disposal of a whole people or of their artisans and their art will be corrupted, not, of course, in all its manifestations, but insofar as it belongs to everyone.

Thus the tragic impasse reached by the modern mind results from the fact that most men are incapable of grasping a priori the compatibility between the symbolic expressions of tradition and the material discoveries established by science; these discoveries stimulate modern man to want to understand the "why" of everything, but he wants this "why" to be as external and as easy as that of "scientific" phenomena; in other words he wants answers on the level of his own experiences; and since these are purely material, his consciousness is closed in advance to all that goes beyond them.

What modern man is no longer willing to admit is above all the idea of an anthropomorphic, "infinitely perfect" God, creating the world "out of goodness" while foreknowing its horrors — creating man "free," while knowing he would make bad use of his freedom; a God who, despite His infinite goodness, would punish man for faults which He, the omniscient Creator, could not fail to foresee. But this is to be hypnotized, quite uselessly, by the inevitable defects of anthropomorphic symbolism, a symbolism which moreover is inevitable and which has been proven to be well-founded by thousands of years of efficacy. It is to contend, not without a certain pretentiousness, against modes of speech which, though no doubt imperfect, are opportune in certain circumstances; and it is to shut oneself off from truth — including even the truth which gives salvation — merely for reasons of dialectic.[1] The answer to these soph-

1. As Saint Peter certainly foresaw: "Knowing this first, that there shall come in the last days scoffers, walking after their own lusts, and saying, Where is the promise of his coming? for since the fathers fell asleep, all things continue as they were from the beginning of the creation" (II Peter 3:3-4).

istries is that the Absolute is not an artificial postulate, explainable by psychology, but a "pre-mental" evidence as actual as the air we breathe or the beating of our hearts; that intelligence when not atrophied — the pure, intuitive, contemplative intellect — allows no doubt on this subject, the "proofs" being in its very substance; that the Absolute of necessity takes on, in relation to man, aspects that are more or less human, without however being intrinsically limited by these aspects; that the possibility of human goodness is metaphysical proof of the divine Goodness, which is necessarily limitless in relation to its earthly traces; that the sentimental anthropomorphism of monotheists is what it has to be, given the character of the masses to which it is addressed; that in a general way the sacred Scriptures, far from being popular tales, are on the contrary highly "scientific" works through their polyvalent symbolism which contains a science at once cosmological, metaphysical and mystical, not forgetting other equally possible applications; that man, when he trusts to his reason alone, only ends by unleashing the dark and dissolving forces of the irrational.

The Vedantic and Buddhist solution, which avoids the obstacles of anthropomorphism, is certainly unsuited to the monotheistic collectivities; however, by a tragic paradox, some answer of this nature has become indispensable to meet the need for causal explanations of these same collectivities once they have lost the religious instinct and have begun wrestling with the logical contradictions anthropomorphism inescapably entails. Such an answer or solution is of necessity to be found also in the West, but in a form in general too indirect to be capable of neutralizing, in the consciousness of the majority, what in anthropotheistic symbolism is ultimately contradictory; most "intellectuals," to speak without euphemism, are not intelligent enough to understand writers like Saint Anselm or Saint Thomas Aquinas, that is to say to understand them in depth and to find there evidence of God. The darkening of our world —

whether we mean the West properly so called or its ramifications in the East and elsewhere — appears patently in the fact that an extreme mental dexterity goes hand in hand with a no less excessive intellectual superficiality; it has become habitual to treat concepts as if they were playthings of the mind, committing one to nothing, in other words everything is touched on and nothing is assimilated; ideas no longer bite into the intelligence, which slides over concepts without taking time to really to grasp them. The modern mind moves "on the surface," all the time playing with mental images, while not knowing their possibilities and role; whereas the traditional mind proceeds in depth, whence come doctrines, which may seem dogmatist, but are fully sufficient and effectual for those who know what a doctrine is. Twentieth century man has lost the sense of repose and contemplation; living on husks, he no longer knows what fruit is like.

One of the great errors of our times is to speak of the "bankruptcy" of religion or the religions; this is to lay blame on truth for our own refusal to admit it; and by the same token it is to deny man both liberty and intelligence. Intelligence depends in large measure on the will, hence on free will, in the sense that free will can contribute towards actualizing intelligence or on the contrary paralyzing it. It was not without reason that medieval theologians located heresy in the will: intelligence can, in fact, fall into error, but its nature does not allow it to resist truth indefinitely; for this to happen it needs the intervention of a factor connected with the will, or, more precisely, with the passions, namely prejudice, sentimental bias, individualism in all its forms. There is, at the basis of every error, an element of irrational "mystique," a tendency not deriving from concepts, but making use of them or producing them: behind every limiting or subversive philosophy can be discerned a "taste" or a "color"; errors proceed from "hardenings," drynesses or intoxications.

Far from proving that modern man "keeps a cool head" and that men of old were dreamers, modern unbelief and "exact science" are to be explained at bottom by a wave of rationalism — sometimes apparently antirationalist — which is reacting against the religious sentimentalism and bourgeois romanticism of the previous epoch; both these tendencies have existed side by side since the "age of reason." The Renaissance also knew such a wave of false lucidity: like our age, it rejected truths along with outworn sentimentalities, replacing them with new sentimentalities that were supposedly "intelligent." To properly understand these oscillations it must be remembered that Christianity as a path of love opposed pagan rationalism; that is to say, it opposed emotional elements possessing a spiritual quality to the implacable, but "worldly," logic of the Greco-Romans, while later on absorbing certain sapiential elements which their civilization comprised.

The essays brought together in this volume doubtless do not give systematic answers to the problems we have just outlined, but they make their contribution to the answer we have tried to give in all our previous works. At a time when the forms of the spirit are threatened as much by man's thoughtlessness as by a preconceived hostility, what is essential is to place in a sapiential setting the truths by which man has always lived and by which he should go on living; if there is an "exact science" embracing all that is, it resides above all in consciousness of the realities underlying both the traditional symbols and the fundamental virtues, which are the "splendor of the true."

Orthodoxy and Intellectuality

At first sight there seems to be no connection between intellectuality and orthodoxy, for the term orthodoxy is too often taken as a synonym of "conformity," even of "prejudice" or "mental laziness," while intellectuality, on the contrary, appears to most of our contemporaries as "unfettered exploration" or even "creative thinking," hence as something at the antipodes of intellectual intuition and contemplation. From our standpoint, orthodoxy is the principle of formal homogeneity proper to any authentically spiritual perspective; it is therefore an indispensable aspect of all genuine intellectuality, which is to say that the essence of every orthodoxy is the truth and not mere fidelity to a system that eventually turns out to be false. To be orthodox means to participate by way of a doctrine that can properly be called "traditional," in the immutability of the principles which govern the Universe and fashion our intelligence.

What perhaps renders somewhat difficult the definition of orthodoxy is that in fact it presents two principal modes, one being essential or intrinsic and the other formal or extrinsic: the latter concerns its accordance with truth in some particular revealed form, the former its accordance with essential and universal truth, whether or not this agrees with a given particular form, so that these two modes may sometimes oppose one another outwardly. For example, Buddhism is on the one hand extrinsically heterodox

1

in relation to Hinduism, because it is separated from the basic forms of the latter, and on the other hand it is intrinsically orthodox because it accords with the universal truth from which it derives. By contrast, the Brahmo-samaj, like every other form of "progressive" neo-Hinduism, is heterodox twice over, firstly in relation to Hinduism and secondly in relation to truth itself, heterodox therefore both from the particular point of view of form and from the universal point of view of essence. A *sannyāsi* may disregard caste without thereby departing from brahmanical orthodoxy, since this orthodoxy recognizes all spiritual possibilities; but if he preaches the abolition of the Hindu social system he is a heretic, for then he is setting himself up against the Revelation, the form "willed by God," or rather one of the forms, for none of them is exclusive. True, the exception proves the rule, that is to say the limitlessness of All-Possibility requires exceptions, and these therefore will occur also in the field of orthodoxy, as is shown by Kabir for example; but here, precisely, the apparent heresy is only on the level of form, without the intrusion of any intrinsically false idea or attitude.[1]

Objections will no doubt be made that Hindu spirituality does not know orthodoxy, since opinions and systems contradict one another in Hinduism even more than in any other traditional wisdom; rightly or wrongly, according to

---

1. Kabir incarnates not a form or a theory, but an essence or a realization; he is the exceptional, but necessary, manifestation of the non-formal link between Hindu *bhakti* and Islamic *mahabbah;* a case such as his could not fail to occur in a place like India which was Brahmanical and Moslem at the same time. In other words, Kabir's *bhakti* is exceptional because it has no formal framework, and it is necessary because dictated by the spiritual circumstances and, above all, by the limitlessness of the divine Possibility. Readers familar with our writings will not be surprised that we like to draw examples from the Hindu world; this world, besides the contemplative character of its peoples and the metaphysical quality of its wisdom, affords a sort of recapitulation or synthesis of all spiritual possibilities, so that we might readily speak of the "miracle of Hinduism."

the individual, it will be claimed that the "great thinkers" of India are beyond forms and so are free from all "narrow dogmatism."[2] It is true that Hindu orthodoxy is sometimes more difficult to grasp from outside than that of a monotheist tradition; this is because Hinduism is founded more directly on the metaphysical essence, so that the form can be treated more freely; also, dogma — or what corresponds to it — assumes forms more varied than in Western religions, which amounts to saying, not that Hinduism is not quite orthodox, but that its orthodoxy has a wider scope in respect of form, which is all that is in question here.[3]

The wide range of forms belonging to Hinduism may be bewildering to some minds, but could never mean that Hinduism sanctions error, as is in fact done by modern philosophy, where "genius" and "culture" count as much as or more than truth, and where the very idea of truth is even called into question by some people. The formal "fluidity" proper to Hinduism in no way prevents error from being always recognizable, whether by the aid of scriptural criteria, or in the light of metaphysical truth, which immediately unmasks absurdity, even when heterodoxy is founded on a sacred text, this of course through falsifying its meaning. The doctrines of *jñāna* and *bhakti* contradict one another outwardly because of the difference of levels and modes, but neither is absurd in itself: to say that the world is unreal, or that it is real, or that it is both at once,

2. Westernized heretics — pseudo-intellectual mollusks if ever there were any — are placed on the same level as the most venerable authorities of the Vedic tradition; the "breadth of mind" boasted by the moderns profits nothing except error and unintelligence.

3. Hinduism, despite its extreme conceptual "elasticity," does not swallow everything, for otherwise Jainism and Buddhism would have become additional *darshanas* [orthodox perspectives] instead of being excluded from specifically Hindu orthodoxy; on the other hand, the very breadth of this orthodoxy allows it to recognize a posteriori — but "on the margin" and without any innovation — the celestial character both of the Buddha and of his message.

or again that it is neither one nor the other, is true according to the perspective adopted, and these perspectives result from objective reality and not from human arbitrariness. Intrinsic heterodoxy is, we repeat, contrary not only to a particular perspective or a particular formulation, but to the very nature of things, for it results, not from a perspective legitimate by nature and therefore "providential," but from the arbitrary judgement of a mind left to its own resources and obliged to "create" what the intellect when paralyzed — fundamentally or accidentally — cannot transmit to it. When a man seeks to escape from dogmatic narrowness it is essential that it be "upwards" and not "downwards": dogmatic form is transcended by fathoming its depths and contemplating its universal content, and not by denying it in the name of a pretentious and iconoclastic ideal of "pure truth."[4]

It is also necessary to take account of the differentiated manifestation of the total doctrine: if "the divergences of theologians are a blessing," as Moslems say, this means that the total doctrine, contained more or less synthetically in the Revelation, is rendered explicit only by "fragments" which are outwardly divergent, although fundamentally concordant. The totality in question here does not relate to the intrinsic truth but to the human possibilities of understanding and realization; it is obvious that in respect of quality the perspective of Shankara, for example, is "total," and that therefore it contains eminently the perspective of Ramanuja, since it goes beyond it: but its formulation could not take account of all possible levels of truth, so that the perspective of Ramanuja becomes necessary. This leads us to point out that an intellectual authority is infallible within the framework assigned to him by the tradition, and on this plane alone; he can assuredly be infallible beyond this

---

4. Within the monotheist religions, sapiential esoterism inevitably presents aspects of extrinsic heterodoxy, for a qualitative difference necessarily shows aspects of opposition.

framework and on all planes, but is not necessarily so, firstly because no man can a priori have knowledge of all the elements of truth, and secondly because intellectual intuition may on occasion operate more easily in one given dimension than in some other, according to the nature of the human receptacle.

When we say that a doctrine is providential, we mean by this that it is contained in its own way in the Revelation itself and that it cannot fail to be "crystallized" at the cyclic moment assigned to it by its nature; thus, *bhakti* has always existed as a spiritual possibility, but its flowering required particular conditions, belonging to a given phase of the Hindu cycle. Every cycle has qualitative aspects: what is possible at a certain moment is not possible at another, so that the birth of a particular perspective cannot occur at some arbitrary moment. And this provides us with yet another criterion of orthodoxy — or of heterodoxy — for it is certain that in our times, that is for the last few centuries, the cyclic moment for the manifestation of the great perspectives *(darshanas)* is past; readaptations — in the sense of a legimate and therefore adequate and efficacious synthesis — are always possible, but not the manifestations of perspectives that are fundamental and "new" as to their form.

The least that can be said is that no present formulation could surpass the ancient formulations; commentaries can be made on the traditional perspectives, they can be summed up from a particular point of view or expressed according to a particular inspiration, but they cannot be contradicted or replaced. It was possible, for example, for Ramanuja to contradict Shankara on the basis of a perspective which, though doubtless limited, was legitimate on its own level and "willed by God"; but no man of our times is a Ramanuja, that is to say there is no one who can reject Shankara except by doing so in the footsteps of Ramanuja and within his doctrinal limits, on the level, that is, of traditional *bhakti;* he could not surpass both Shankara's *jnāna* and Ramanuja's *bhakti* at the same time, claiming to classify them and to add to them a new and better element. The spuriousness of such attempts always shows itself — apart from intrinsic errors — in the belittling and falsifying spirit which is so characteristic of the modern world; in fact it requires a prodigious lack of spiritual sensibility and of a sense of proportion to take any contemporary thinking, even the best possible, for one of the great providential "crystallizations" of the *philosophia perennis*.

*

* *

This question of the limitations of Ramanuja's outlook — or of *bhakti* in general — obliges us to point out that in order to avoid some quite unjustifiable confusions, a distinction must be made between two degrees of doctrinal limitation which are eminently unequal: in the first case the doctrine comprises certain restrictions in view of particular mental conditions or a particular spiritual method; in the second case it is intrinsically false; there lies the whole difference between lesser truth and error. The first limitation is to some extent dictated by the needs of a particular mentality, and is thus "willed by God" — whether it is a question of Ramanuja or of Aristotle, to cite two very different cases — whereas the second arises from human weakness and also from the devil, who exploits this weakness, and who cannot but exploit it. In other words, two doctrines may be opposed to one another either because of a legitimate difference of perspective,[5] or because one of them is

5. When Averroes asserts the unity of the intellect and apparently seems to deny the immortality of the individual soul, he is right in the sense that the one, universal Intellect exists — particular intelligences being luminous thanks to it alone — and that the purely sentient part of the soul is in fact perishable; but his opponents also are right in the sense that the diversification of the intelligence and the immortality of the human person are incontestable realities. The specifically philosophical

erroneous, or because both are so but in different ways; care must therefore be taken to avoid putting oppositions of form on the same level with fundamental contradictions.

It is not possible to emphasize too strongly that philosophy, in its humanistic and rationalizing and therefore current sense, consists primarily of logic; this definition of Guénon's correctly situates philosophical thought in making clear its distinction from "intellectual intuition," which is direct perception of truth. But another distinction must also be established on the rational plane itself: logic can either operate in accordance with an intellection or on the contrary put itself at the disposal of an error, so that philosophy can become the vehicle of just about anything; it may be an aristotelianism conveying ontological knowledge, just as it may degenerate into an existentialism in which logic is no more than a blind, unreal activity, and which can rightly be described as an "esoterism of stupidity."[6] When unintelligence — and what we mean by this is in no way incompatible with "worldly" intelligence — joins with passion to prostitute logic, it is impossible to escape a mental satanism which destroys the very bases of intelligence and truth.

The validity of a logical demonstration depends then on the prior knowledge which this demonstration aims at communicating, and it is clearly false to take as the point of departure, not a direct cognition, but logic pure and simple; when man has no "visionary" — as opposed to discursive — knowledge of Being, and when he thinks only with his brain instead of "seeing" with the "heart," all his logic will be useless to him, since he starts from an initial blind-

---

or logical point of view — apart from all question of spiritual opportuneness — is characterized by its incapacity to reconcile antinomic truths, an incapacity deriving from the very nature of reason.

6. What is to be said of a system of "metaphysics" which ponderously places human experience at the centre of reality — as if our intelligence did not allow us to go further — and which operates with concepts as grossly subjective and conjectural as "anxiety" and "anguish"?

ness. A further distinction must be made between the validity of a demonstration and its dialectical efficacy; the latter evidently depends on an intuitive disposition for recognizing the truth demonstrated, namely on intellectual capacity, which amounts to saying that a demonstration is effective for those to whom it applies. Logic is nothing other than the science of mental coordination, of rational conclusion; hence it cannot attain to the universal and the transcendent by its own resources; a supra-logical — but not "illogical" — dialectic based on symbolism and on analogy, and therefore descriptive rather than ratiocinative, may be harder for some people to assimilate, but it conforms more closely to transcendent realities. Avant-garde philosophy is properly an acephalous logic: it labels what is intellectually evident as "prejudice"; seeking to free itself from the servitudes of the mind, it falls into infra-logic; closing itself, above, to the light of the intellect, it opens itself, below, to the darkness of the subconscious.[7] Philosophical scepticism takes itself for an absence of prejudices and a healthy attitude, whereas it is something quite artificial: it is a result not

7. This is what Kant with his rationalistic ingenuousness did not foresee. According to him, every cognition which is not rational in the narrowest sense, is mere pretentiousness and fanciful enthusiasm *(Schwärmerei);* now, if there is anything pretentious it is this very opinion. Phantasy, arbitrariness and irrationality are not features of the Scholastics, but they certainly are of the rationalists who persist in violently contesting, with ridiculous and often pathetic arguments, everything which eludes their grasp. With Voltaire, Rousseau and Kant, bourgeois (or *vaishya,* as the Hindus would say) unintelligence is put forward as a "doctrine" and definitively installed in European "thought," giving birth — by way of the French Revolution — to scientism, industry and to quantitative "culture." Mental hypertrophy in the "cultured" man henceforth compensates the absence of intellectual penetration; the sense of the absolute and the principial is drowned in a mediocre empiricism, coupled with a pseudo-mysticism posing as "positive" or "human." Some people may reproach us with a lack of due consideration, but we would ask what due consideration is shown by philosophers who shamelessly slash down the wisdom of countless centuries.

of knowledge but of ignorance, and that is why it is as contrary to intelligence as it is to reality.

The fact that the philosophic mode of thought is centered on logic and not directly on intuition implies that intuition is left at the mercy of logic's needs: in Scholastic disputations it was a question of avoiding certain truths which, given the general level of mentality, might have given rise to certain dangerous conclusions. Scholasticism, it should be remembered, is above all a defense against error: its aim is to be an apologetic and not, as in the case of "metaphysically operative" doctrines — gnosis or *jñāna* — a support for meditation and contemplation. Before Scholasticism, Greek philosophy had also aimed to satisfy a certain need for causal explanations rather than to furnish the intelligence with a means of realization; moreover, the disinterested character of truth easily becomes, on the level of speculative logic, a tendency towards "art for art's sake," whence the *ventosa loquacitas philosophorum* stigmatized by Saint Bernard. Some will certainly raise the objection that traditional metaphysics, whether of the East or the West, makes use of rational argumentations like any philosophy; but an argumentation a man uses to describe to his fellow men what he knows is one thing, and one that he uses on himself because he knows nothing is quite another. This is a crucial distinction, for it marks the whole difference between the intellectual "visionary" and the mere "thinker" who "gropes alone through the darkness" (Descartes) and whose pride it is to deny that there could be any knowledge which does not proceed in the same fashion.

*

* *

The intellect is a receptive faculty and not a productive power: it does not "create," it receives and transmits; it is a mirror reflecting reality in a manner that is adequate and therefore effective. In most men of the "iron age" the intellect is atrophied to the point of being reduced to a mere virtuality, although doubtless there is no watertight partition between it and the reason, for a sound process of reasoning indirectly transmits something of the intellect; be that as it may, the respective operations of the reason — or the mind — and of the intellect are fundamentally different from the point of view that interests us here, despite certain appearances due to the fact that every man is a thinking being, whether he be wise or ignorant. There is at the same time analogy and opposition: the mind is analogous to the intellect insofar as it is a kind of intelligence, but is opposed to it by its limited, indirect and discursive character; as for the apparent limitations of the intellect, they are merely accidental and extrinsic, while the limits of the mental faculty are inherent in it. Even if the intellect cannot exteriorize the "total truth" — or rather reality — because that is in itself impossible, it can perfectly well establish points of reference which are adequate and sufficient, rather as it is possible to represent space by a circle, a cross, a square, a spiral or a point, and so on. Truth and reality must not be confused: the latter relates to "being" and signifies the aseity of things, and the former relates to "knowing" — to the image of reality reflected in the mirror of the intellect — and signifies the adequation of "being" and "knowing"; it is true that reality is often designated by the word "truth," but this is a dialectical synthesis which aims at defining truth in relation to its virtuality of "being," of "reality." If truth is thus made to embrace ontological reality, aseity, the inexpressible, and so also the "personal" realization of the Divine, there is clearly no "total truth" on the plane of thought; but if by "truth" is understood thought insofar as it is an adequate reflection, on the intellectual plane, of "being," there is a "total truth" on this plane, but on condition firstly that nothing quantitative is envisaged in this totality, and secondly that it is made clear that this totality can have a relative sense, according to the order of thought to which it belongs. There is a total truth which is such because it embraces, in principle, all possible truths: this is metaphysical doctrine, whether its enunciation be simple or complex, symbolical or dialectical; but there is also a truth which is total on the plane of spiritual realization, and in this case "truth" becomes synonymous with "reality." Since on the plane of facts there is never anything absolute — or more precisely, nothing "absolutely absolute" — the "totality," while being perfect and sufficient in practice, is always relative in theory; it is indefinitely extensible, but also indefinitely reducible; it can assume the form of an extended doctrine, but also that of a simple sentence, just as the totality of space can be expressed by a system of interwining patterns too complex for the eye to unravel, but also by an elementary geometrical figure.

We have compared pure intelligence to a mirror; now it must be recalled that there is always a certain element of inversion in the relationship between subject and object, that is, the subject which reflects inverts the object reflected. A tree reflected in water is inverted, and so is "false" in relation to the real tree, but it is still a tree — even "this" tree — and never anything else: consequently the reflected tree is perfectly "true," despite its illusory character, so that it is a mistake to conclude that intellection is illusory because of its subjective framework. The powers of the cosmic illusion are not unlimited, for the Absolute is reflected in the contingent, otherwise the latter would not exist; everything is in God — "All is *Ātmā*" — and the Absolute flashes forth everywhere, it is "infinitely close"; barriers are illusory, they are at the same time immeasurably great and infinitesimally small. The world is antinomic by definition, which is a way of saying it is not God; every image is at the same time true and false, and it suffices to discern the various relationships. Christ is "true God and true man," which is the very formula of the antinomy and parallelism governing the cosmos: antinomy because the creature is not the Creator, and parallelism because nothing can be "outside God," Reality being one.

In a certain sense, doctrine is identical with truth, for account must always be taken of the "relatively absolute"; doctrine should have more than a relative value for us, seeing that its content transcends relativities to the extent that it is essential. There is no difficulty in the fact that pure intelligence — the intellect — immensely surpasses thought, and that there is no continuity — despite the identity of essence — between a concept as such and reality, the aseity of the real; to lament over the shortcomings of thought is to ask it to be something that it is not; this is the classical error of philosophers who seek to enclose everything in the *cogito* alone. From the point of view of concrete — not abstract — knowledge of the transcendent, the problem of thought is resolved in the very nature of the intellect.

There are objects which exceed the possibilities of reason; there are none which exceed those of intelligence as such. If there were not something absolute in man — he is "made in the image of God" — he would be only an animal like other animals; but man knows the animals, while they do not know man. Man alone can step out of the cosmos, and this possibility proves — and presupposes — that in a certain way he incarnates the Absolute.[8]

*

* *

Intellectual intuition implies, among other things, the comprehension of Being, both in itself and in connection with things; this intuition therefore allows of understanding on the one hand that Being does not have to be defined at every turn to satisfy an artificial need for causality, and on the other that Being is in no way difficult to define, pre-

---

8. Without this quality of absoluteness there could be no question either of his salvation or of his damnation.

cisely because the sense of Being is inherent in the intellect; to say "intellect" is to say "sense of Being."

In connection with this question of intellectual intuition, it would be useful to reply here to a difficulty raised by Pascal: "One cannot undertake to define being without falling into absurdity: for a word cannot be defined without beginning with the words *it is*, whether they are expressed or implied. Therefore in order to define being it would be necessary to say *it is*, and so to use the word to be defined in formulating its own definition" *(Pensées et Opuscules).*[9] It is in fact impossible, in European languages, to give a definition without using the word "is"; if in other languages, in Arabic for example, a definition can be made without the help of this word or of some other copulative, that is exactly for the same reason, namely that all is immersed in Being and that Being therefore has an a priori evidentness; if Being cannot be defined outside itself, any more than can Knowledge, it is because this "outside" does not exist; the separation necessary for every definition thus actually lies within the thing to be defined, and in fact although we are "within Being" we are not Being. The copulative "it is" indicates a determination or an attribute according to the circumstances, and this shows the meaning of the word: we will define Being in itself as the universal determination, that is to say as the supreme Principle "insofar as It determines itself," to use Guénon's expression; if we start from the ternary Beyond-Being, Being and Manifestation, we see that Being is "Principle" in relation to the world but "determination" in relation to Beyond-Being.[10] Now, given that Being is determination in relation

9. Beyond-Being — or Non-Being — is Reality absolutely unconditioned, while Being is Reality insofar as It determines Itself in the direction of its manifestation and in so doing becomes personal God.

10. The French *Sur-Etre* has generally been translated throughout by the phrase "Beyond-Being" rather than by "Supra-Being," since the latter might convey the idea of a superior level of Being instead of that of the Reality which transcends Being altogether. (Translator's note)

to Beyond-Being and the source of every attribute in relation to the world, every determination and every attribute can be expressed by means of the verb "to be," hence by "it is," so that Pascal's difficulty can be resolved thus: "*being*" manifests (or "is" the manifestation of) an aspect of its own inner limitlessness, thus a possibility, an attribute. When we say: "The tree is green," this is, by analogy, like saying: "Being comprises such and such an aspect," or again in the deepest sense: "Beyond-Being determines itself as Being"; the thing to be defined — or determined — serves analogically as "Being," and the definition — the determination — serves as "divine attribute." Instead of speaking of "Being" and of "attribute of Being," we could refer to the first distinction: Beyond-Being and Being. When the verb "to be" designates an existence, it has no complement; on the other hand, when it has a complement it does not designate an existence as such, but an attribute; to say that a certain thing "is," signifies that it is not non-existent; to say that the tree "is green" signifies that it has this attribute and not some other. In consequence, the verb "to be" always expresses either an "existence" or a "character of existence," in the same way as God on the one hand "is" and on the other "is thus," that is to say Light, Love, Power and so forth. Saint Thomas expresses this well by saying that if Being and the first principles which flow from it are incapable of proof, it is because they have no need of proof; to prove them is at once useless and impossible, "not through a lack, but through a superabundance of light."[11]

11. In the *Cogito ergo sum* all is lost, since consciousness of being is subordinated to the experience of thought; when being is thus blurred it carries thought downwards with it, for if it is necessary to prove being, it is necessary also to prove the efficacy of the intelligence, hence the validity of its conclusions, the soundness of the *ergo*. Guénon, who had the great merit of restoring to the conceptions of intellectuality and of orthodoxy their true and universal meaning, once wrote to us on the subject of the *Cogito:* "In order to see all that is involved in Descartes' saying 'I think, therefore I am,' it is necessary to consider the twofold

When intellectual intuition is operative, there is no problem of Being, and enunciations considered to be "summary" and "dogmatic" are in fact sufficient; but when the intellect is paralyzed, every effort to define Being is vain, for it is obvious that one cannot define what one does not know. If for some people today the idea of "being" is "the most obscure there is," this is certainly nothing to cause surprise; but what is disturbing is when blindness poses as light, or as "leading to light," which amounts to the same thing. Intellectual intuition cannot be created where it is absent from the essence of the individual, but it can be actualized where its absence is only accidental, otherwise it would be senseless to speak of it; knowledge, as Saint Augustine maintains with Plato and many others, is not something that is added from outside; teaching is only the occasional cause of the grasping of a truth already latent within us. Teaching is a recalling; understanding is a recollection. In the intellect, the subject is the object, "being," and the object is the subject, "knowing": whence comes absolute certitude.

reduction which this effects: firstly, the 'I' is reduced to the soul alone (the body being excluded); and secondly, the soul itself is reduced to thought, 'a substance the whole nature of which consists solely of thinking'; the distinction which he maintains between substances and their respective principal attributes seems to be primarily verbal since for him the principal attribute expresses completely the essence or the nature of the substance. There has been much discussion on the question of knowing whether the Cartesian formula ought really to be considered as an argument or line of reasoning; the *ergo* however does not seem open to any interpretation other than as signifying a deduction. The same objection can also be applied to the famous 'ontological argument'; everything that it contains which is true and metaphysically valid comes down to the affirmation 'Being is,' where there is no trace of argument. In this connection one could recall the absurd philosophical question of the 'criterion of truth,' that is to say the search for an external sign by which truth would infallibly be recognized; this question is among those that cannot be solved because they do not really arise."

Metaphysical truth cannot be regarded as having, by definition, solely a character of complexity, even of difficulty; everything depends on our "visual capacity" and the angle from which we approach the transcendent realities. Things apparently most complex and difficult are from a certain point of view simple and easy, because the Essence is simple, provided one's intelligence goes beyond the resources of the discursive mind and has the ability to grasp the real in depth. If truth is accessible, it has an aspect of facility; if it is inaccessible, it is useless to speak of it; truth would not then be a human notion. To be so over-prudent as to believe only in the complex is a failure to see that the Absolute simplifies: in fact, wherever the Absolute is "incarnate" it manifests an aspect of simplicity, which one must beware of wanting to water down in human relativities — of a psychological or historical kind for example — as if intelligence were bound to complicate the simple while at the same time debasing the sublime. There cannot be an "absolutely relative," but there is a "relatively absolute" by virtue of which essential determinations maintain all their rigor on the relative plane, at least in respect of their qualitative content, which is all that matters in the cases to be considered. All relativism applied to the intelligence as such — or to the truth — is radically false, and this falsity already results from the inner contradiction which all "intellectual" relativism implies; for on what grounds would it be possible to judge when one denies, implicitly or explicitly, the possibility of objective judgement, thus of judgement as such? If the intelligence possesses the faculty of transcending the human level, of getting outside the vicious circle of thinking, of defining its own mechanism from a "neutral" starting-point, then it has always possessed this faculty; if it does not possess it, then it is not possible for philosophers — any more than for others — to throw any light on this subject, on pain of contradiction, and all their subtleties prove empty.

The principle of simplicity just mentioned, which is not other than a certain reflection of the Absolute, nullifies every objection that philosophical speculation — which is "mental" and not "intellective" — is able to advance against the imperative character of the truth. All expression is of necessity relative, but language is nonetheless capable of conveying the quality of absoluteness which has to be conveyed; expression contains all, like a seed; it opens all, like a master-key; what remains to be seen is to which capacity of understanding it is addressed. Doctrine offers the whole truth, first by virtue of its form, and then in regard to the capacity of the properly qualified intelligence to receive and actualize it; it lays open its content in a way that is doubtless elliptical, since it is a form, but in a way that is also total since this form is a symbol and is therefore something of what it has to communicate. The accidental — but not essential — discontinuity between content and expression will make no difference; we observe it, since it exists in the respect envisaged, but practically speaking it does not concern us. The discernment between the accidental and the essential is a basic function of the intelligence; the latter is a direct "consciousness," a non-formal essence, against which it is of no avail for the discursive mind to try to lay down the law, should the occasion arise. If our knowledge cannot be certain, it is idle to think; if it can be certain, that proves we can have all the certainty there is.

If there were no points at which the incommensurable complexity of the real — or of the unreal — became quite simple, quite tangible, we would have no possibility of contact with truth. Relative, indirect knowledge of the Absolute is "essentially" — that is to say insofar as it is knowledge, not insofar as it is relative — absolute, direct knowledge; everything lies in grasping the mental symbol in its center or in its essence. This precisely is a characteristic aspect of

17

Taoism and of Zen: what is infinitely far off is also infinitely close. One man can spend his whole life in searching and looking, and still know nothing, "see" nothing; another may arrive without trouble at intellectual certainties, and this proves that his ignorance was only accidental and not fundamental. Likewise with sanctity: there is no common measure between efforts and results; enlightenment means to awaken into the infinite Consciousness which is certitude, totality, reality; a degree of enlightenment is always in some measure total Consciousness, for there are no hard and fast barriers here; intellectual intuition lies along the axis centered on the Absolute. Between a doctrinal concept and infinite Consciousness there is no continuity, despite the analogy which indicates an essential identity; this is what the scrutinizers of "human thought" are incapable of conceiving, and that is why they expect to obtain everything on the level of words. A symbol is relative and absolute at the same time, like the intellect; it is necessary to understand and realize the absoluteness and thus burn up the accidentality. Criticism by discursive thought is an endless task since the contingent is inexhaustible, and it is erroneous since the contingent cannot be discerned and defined in its total nature except by reference to the Absolute; this Absolute we rejoin in pure Consciousness. Intellectual intuition is a participation in this state; if there were no microcosmic anticipation of infinite Consciousness no knowledge would be possible, still less any realization, any gnosis, that is to say effective, "existential" knowledge.[12]

The discontinuity between concept and Reality is compensated and as it were abolished by the identity existing between them: in this second relationship, which metaphys-

12. This word, which we use here in a quite provisional way, is inaccurate inasmuch as transcendent knowledge goes beyond Existence and can even go beyond Being. In the letter from which we have already quoted, Guénon emphazises that "for metaphysics, the use of rational argument never represents more than a mode of outward expression (necessarily

ically is crucial, the idea "is" the Truth. In order to see here a kind of continuity it would in any case be necessary to specify that it is a purely essential, not "material" or "physical" continuity, and therefore not subject to any possible individual experience; this reservation means, not that the experience cannot occur in the domain of the intellect, but that it cannot occur on the mental plane, which is that of the individual as such.

*

* *

If it is useless to seek to establish a "system" embracing every possible aspect of Truth or Reality, it is nonetheless legitimate to develop a traditional perspective to the point of drawing from it all the consequences that human experience can require, and such development will in principle be unlimited. If there can be no exhaustive system of the real, for example, of the intelligible nature of the world, it is because there can be no total coincidence between reality and its reflection in the logical order, otherwise the two would be indistinguishable. However, when there is knowledge of the metaphysical basis from which a given system proceeds, this system can furnish all the keys needed to the reality concerned.

Insofar as the quality of systematization is a perfection, God is systematic — He is a "Geometer" — and so is the truth; but insofar as a system is a limitation, the truth escapes all systematization. Concretely, this means that every traditional doctrine has an aspect of system and an aspect of indeterminacy; this latter appears in the variety of orthodox perspectives, hence also in the plurality of sys-

imperfect and inadequate as such) and in no way affects metaphysical knowledge itself, for the latter must always be kept essentially distinct from its formulation; and formulation, whatever form it may assume, can never be taken as anything but a symbol of that which in itself is incommunicable."

tems, such as may appear in the writings of one and the same author, above all in the esoteric field.

In any case it is absurd to want to exploit for the benefit of heterodoxy — and so of freedom for error — scriptural passages like the following: "The Vedas are divided. . . . There is no sage whose thought is not divided. . . ." Such texts, far from evincing a more or less agnostic relativism, do no more than state the principle of limitation, of exclusion, of contradiction and division implied in every affirmation. "Why callest thou me good? There is none good but one, that is, God," said Christ; which signifies that every manifestation, even if divine, implies imperfection; it implies it because it is manifestation, and not on account of its content, since the latter may be divine, and therefore "absolute." If a Taoist master could say that "only error is transmitted," it is because there is an inverse relationship between "idea" and "reality," the "thought" and the "lived," the "conceived" and the "realized"; this is the application of the principle which Sufis call "isthmus" *(barzakh)*: seen from above the symbol is darkness, but seen from below, it is light. This inversion, however, is not everything, for there is also direct analogy, essential identity, otherwise there would be no symbolism to provide a framework for the wisdom of the sages; to show the earthly or human side — an inevitable side — of tradition is by no means to destroy tradition.

It was pointed out above that the intellect, which is a mirror, must not be confused with spiritual realization, thanks to which our being, and not merely our thought, participates in the objects which the mirror reflects. The mirror is horizontal, while realization is vertical; the vertical ascent certainly purifies the mirror, but the mirror must adequately reflect the essential outlines of the archetypes, otherwise the ascent is impossible. The goal of spiritual realization cannot go beyond the span of the field of vision, just as in an equilateral triangle the height of the apex depends on the length of the base; bhaktic doctrine cannot lead as if by chance to the goal envisaged by *jñāna;* an anthropomorphic and individualist "mythology" or a "passional" mysticism excludes a final objective lying beyond the cosmic realm. But the distinction between the intellect and spiritual realization should make us understand above all that, if intellectual intuition implies absolute certainty, it does not however exclude the possibility of error on a plane of insufficiently known facts, unless these facts fall directly within the "jurisdiction" of the intellectual mode in question; this question has already been referred to in connection with authority. Every manifestation of absoluteness — and the authority flowing from intellectual intuition is one such — presupposes an appropriate framework: "the perfect man" — said a Buddhist master — "may be uninformed on secondary matters of which he has no experience, but he can never be wrong on what his power of discernment has already revealed to him. . . . He knows clay, but he has not acquired knowledge of every form that clay can be given." On the other hand it must not be forgotten that, as was mentioned above, intellectual intuition may operate only within certain "dimensions" of the spirit, according to given modes or within given domains; the intelligence may be centered on some particular aspect of the real. The drawbacks which may result from such differences are however neutralized, in the broadest sense, by the traditional framework, which offers to each predisposition its appropriate field.

In short, there are three essential causes of error; lack of intelligence, lack of information and lack of virtue, that is to say of beauty, in the receptacle. In the first case, the defect is in the subject: the intelligence is neutralized by an internal impediment, either essential or accidental or acquired; in the second case, the defect lies with the object: the intelligence has no possibility of operating adequately because the necessary data are missing; in the third case, the defect is on the periphery of the intellective subject: the intelligence is then reduced, not in its actual essence, but in its modes of operation, which are burdened or falsified by the intervention of passional elements, whether of a hardening or of a dissipating nature. Unintelligence and vice may be merely superficial, that is, to some extent accidental and so curable, just as they may be relatively "essential" and in practice incurable; an essential lack of virtue however is incompatible with transcendent intelligence, just as a very high degree of virtue is scarcely to be found in a fundamentally unintelligent being.[13]

When error is attributed to a lack of intelligence, it means that this lack may by nature be either "vertical" or "horizontal": leaving aside mere stupidity, we would say that intelligence may be extremely acute on the rational level alone, while being quite inoperative beyond that level; or again, it may be penetrating even in the sphere of pure metaphysics, but lacking "breadth" in the sense that it is incapable, in practice though not in principle, of grasping certain aspects of things or certain dimensions of reality; in other words, intelligence may be limited not only as to degree, but also as to mode, though this does not compromise it on the plane of its particular competence.

*

* *

We cannot insist too strongly on the following: if the relative did not comprise something of the absolute, relativities could not be distinguished qualitatively from one another. It is clearly not as a relativity that orthodoxy gives salvation, but by virtue of its quality of absoluteness; Revelation is infallible light insofar as it is the divine Subject

---

13. Lack of mental cleverness does not exclude sharpness of understanding; the Curé d'Ars, contrary to widespread opinion, was very far from being dull-witted; conversely, experience proves only too cruelly that mental cleverness may not go hand in hand with intelligence, which amounts to saying that it has not in itself any relationship with true intellectuality.

objectivized, but not insofar as it is objectification pure and simple. Revelation, tradition, orthodoxy and intellectual intuition would be inconceivable but for the qualitative and quasi-absolute element which is present at the center and in the arteries of the cosmos, and which flashes forth to produce the phenomenon of the sacred.

In philosophical relativism, there is obviously no place for the concept of the relatively absolute, nor consequently for that of qualitative differences; if relativism were right, the world would be a mere amorphous substance. The relativist position could be compared with the following reasonings: the color white is not light, hence there is only a quantitative difference between black and white; the expression of truth is not truth itself, hence there is only a quantitative — or let us say relative — difference between expressed truth and error.[14] Under these conditions, all qualitative determinations disappear in a shadow-land of relativism; when the truth becomes thus diluted in a sort of universal error, every spiritual value quits the scene, and there remains nothing but a satanic game — satanic because illusory and leading nowhere — a game played with half-truths of an ever more arbitrary ingenuity. It is as

14. To see things in this way means that there would be no difference between the discussions of the Hindu schools for example and those of modern philosophers; in reality the difference is radical owing to the fact that the Hindus were subject in a direct manner to a tradition, to an orthodoxy which they sought to affirm in the best possible way, a fact which serves as a guarantee of inspiration, whereas the moderns on the contrary engage in discussions based on their concern to escape every "preconceived idea," whence their rejection of all orthodoxy, all "dogmatism," all scriptural criteria. Similarly, people fail to see any essential difference between traditional civilizations and modern civilization, on the pretext that the former involved evils like the latter, whereas there is no common measure between a civilization which "is" an evil by its very principle, and another which, while being good, "includes" in fact some inevitable evils. Christianity as such is in the same situation as other traditions; but modernism precisely is not Christianity, it is not an "ailing religion" but an "anti-religion."

if discernment, having turned away from qualitative determinations — by which we mean everything that reflects the Absolute in whatever manner — had henceforth been eager to introduce scissions in the intelligence itself. Thus relativism mixes together things that are in reality different and differentiates what is simple; objectively, it abolishes the qualitative hierarchies — it eliminates the absolute element from the relative — and subjectively, by a compensatory movement, it dissects the adequation which knowledge constitutes, and this amounts to denying the latter's efficacy. Relativism, even when it makes a show of admitting the interventions of an absolute in the relative, gives them such a quantitative air as to take away precisely their absoluteness; it seeks to destroy either the idea of truth, or that of intelligence, or both at once. To lend a relative character to what functionally stands for the absolute is to attribute absoluteness to the relative; to claim that knowledge as such can only be relative amounts to saying that human ignorance is absolute; to throw doubt on certitude is, logically, to avow that one knows "absolutely" nothing."[15]

Wearied by the artifices and the lack of imagination of academic rationalism, many of our contemporaries in rejecting it reject true metaphysics as well, because they think it "abstract" — which in their minds is synonymous with "artificial" — and seek the "concrete," not beyond the rational and in the order of ontological prototypes, but in crude fact, in the sensory, the "actual"; man becomes the arbitrary measure of everything, and thereby abdicates his dignity as man, namely his possibility of objective and universal knowledge. He is then the measure of things not in a truly human but in an animal way; his dull empiricism is that of an animal which registers facts and notices a pasture or a path; but since he is despite all a "human animal," he

---

15. In every field, it is "absoluteness" which creates quality; thus a work of art is not concerned with registering accidents; it must touch upon essences.

disguises his dullness in mental arabesques. The existential-
ists are human as it were by chance; what distinguishes them
from animals is not human intelligence but the human style
of an infra-human intelligence.

The protagonists of "concrete" thought, of whatever
shade, readily label as "speculations in the abstract" whatever goes beyond their understanding, but they forget to
tell us why these speculations are possible, that is to say what
confers this strange possibility on human intelligence. Thus
what does it mean that for thousands of years men deemed
to be wise have practiced such speculations, and by what
right does one call "intellectual progress" the replacement
of these speculations by a crude empiricism which excludes
on principle any operation characteristic of intelligence? If
these "positivists" are right, none but they are intelligent;
all the founders of religions, all the saints, all the sages have
been wrong on essentials whereas Mr. So-and-So at long last
sees things clearly; one might just as well say that human
intelligence does not exist. There are those who claim that
the idea of God is to be explained only by social opportun-
ism, without taking account of the infinite disproportion
and the contradiction involved in such a hypothesis; if such
men as Plato, Aristotle or Thomas Aquinas — not to mention the Prophets, or Christ or the sages of Asia — were not
capable of noticing that God is merely a social prejudice or
some other dupery of the kind, and if hundreds and thousands of years have been based intellectually on their incapacity, then there is no human intelligence, and still less any
possibility of progress, for a being absurd by nature does
not contain the possibility of ceasing to be absurd.

*
* *

In order to get a firm grasp of the dominant tendencies
of contemporary philosophy it is important to note the
following: everything which does not derive either from
intellectual intuition or from revelation is of necessity a

form of "rationalism," because man disposes of no other resource outside the intellect. One criterion of rationalism, even when disguised, is thinking in alternatives, which results from the fact that spanning antinomical realities is beyond the scope of reason; reason has no consciousness of analogies which exceed its radius of action, even though it is aware of them through their reflections on the physical plane; the discursive mind, beyond a certain level, sees only "segments" and not the "circle." Let us say at once that a consciously rationalizing thought, the content of which is true, is worth infinitely more than an anti-rationalist reaction which only ends in destroying the ideas of intelligence and truth: rationalism properly so called is false not because it seeks to express reality in rational mode, so far as this is possible, but because it seeks to embrace the whole of reality in the reason, as if the latter coincided with the very principle of things. In other words, rationalism does not present itself as a possible — and necessarily relative — development of a traditional and sapiential point of view, but it usurps the function of pure intellectuality. But there are degrees to be observed here, as for example with Aristotle: his fundamental ideas — like those of "form" and "matter" (hylomorphism) — really flow from a metaphysical knowledge, and so from supra-mental intuition; they carry in themselves all the universal significance of symbols and become rational — and therefore "abstract" — only to the extent that they become encrusted in a more or less artificial system.

There is a close relationship between rationalism and modern science; the latter is at fault not in concerning itself solely with the finite, but in seeking to reduce the Infinite to the finite, and consequently in taking no account of Revelation, an attitude which is, strictly speaking, inhuman; what we reproach modern science for is that it is inhuman — or infra-human — and not that it has no knowledge of the facts which it studies, even though it deliberately ignores certain of their modalities. It believes that it is possible to approach total knowledge of the world — which after all is indefinite — by what can only be a finite series of discoveries, as if it were possible to exhaust the inexhaustible. And what is to be said of the pretentiousness which sets out to "discover" the ultimate causes of existence, or of the intellectual bankruptcy of those who seek to subject their philosophy to the results of scientific research? A science of the finite cannot legitimately occur outside a spiritual tradition, for intelligence is prior to its objects, and God is prior to man; an experiment which ignores the spiritual link characterizing man no longer has anything human about it; it is thus in the final analysis as contrary to our interests as it is to our nature; and "ye shall know them by their fruits." A science of the finite has need of a wisdom which goes beyond it and controls it, just as the body needs a soul to animate it, and the reason an intellect to illumine it. The "Greek miracle" with its so-called "liberation of the human spirit" is in reality nothing but the beginning of a purely external knowledge, cut off from genuine *Sophia*.[16]

16. It is said that Einstein, for example, revolutionized the vision of the world as Galileo or Newton had done before him, and that the usual conceptions which he overturned — those of space, time, light and matter — are "as naive as those of the Middle Ages"; but then there is nothing to guarantee that his theory of relativity will not be judged naive in its turn, so that, in profane science, it is never possible to escape the vicious circle of "naivety." Moreover, what could be more naive than to seek to enclose the Universe in a few mathematical formulae, and then to be surprised to find that there always remains an elusive and apparently "irrational" element which evades all attempts to "bring it to heel"? We shall no doubt be told that not all scientists are atheists, but this is not the question, since atheism is inherent in science itself, in its postulates and its methods. The Einsteinian theories on mass, space and time are of a nature to demonstrate the fissures in the physical universe, but only a metaphysician can profit from them; science unconsciously provides keys, but is incapable of making use of them, because intellectuality cannot be replaced by something outside itself. The theory of relativity illustrates of necessity certain aspects of metaphysics, but does not of itself

A striking feature of modern science is the disproportion between the scientific, mathematical, practical intelligence and intelligence as such: a scientist may be capable of the most extraordinary calculations and achievements but may at the same time be incapable of understanding the ultimate causality of things. This amounts to an illegitimate and monstrous disproportion, for the man who is intelligent enough to grasp nature in its deepest physical aspects, ought also to know that nature has a metaphysical Cause which transcends it, and that this Cause does not confine itself to determining the laws of sensory existence, as Spinoza claimed. What we have called the inhuman character of modern science also appears in the monstrous fruits it produces, such as the overpopulation of the globe, the degeneration of humankind, and, by compensation, the means of mass destruction.

Rationalism properly so called had, despite all, the merit of not being purely and simply subject to the investigations of science, hence to material facts; it still kept a certain awareness of the dignity of the intelligence confronting the vicissitudes of experience. But thought in its most specifically modern form destroys intelligence itself, so that nothing remains but the establishing of facts, often arbitrarily selected and isolated from their indispensable context, and then interpreted in such manner as to destroy what consti-

open up any higher perspective; the way in which Euclidean geometry is improperly relativized goes to prove this. On the one hand the philosophical point of view trespasses on science, and on the other the scientific point of view trespasses on metaphysics. As for the Einsteinian postulate of a transmathematical absolute, this absolute is not supra-conscious: it is not therefore more than ourselves and could not be the Cause of our intelligence; Einstein's "God" remains blind just as his relativized universe remains physical: one might as well say that it is nothing. Modern science has nothing it can tell us — and this not by accident but by principle — about the miracle of consciousness and all that is connected with it, from the most minute particles of consciousness to be found in creation up to the pure and trans-personal Intellect.

tutes the very value of the human state; the human spirit is denied the faculty of objectivity and universality, as if, in these conditions, there still remained something to be thought.

*

* *

A few words must be said here on the antinomy between dogmatism and empiricism: the empiricist error consists not in the belief that experiment has a certain utility, which is obvious, but in thinking that there is a common measure between principial knowledge and experiment, and in attributing to the latter an absolute value, whereas in fact it can only have a bearing on modes, never on the very principles of Intellect and of Reality; this amounts to purely and simply denying the possibility of a knowledge other than the experimental and sensory. On the dogmatist side, on the contrary, it is necessary to guard against the danger of underestimating the role of experiment within the limits where it is valid, for even thought based on an awareness of principles can go astray on the level of applications, and that precisely through ignorance of certain possible modes, without such misapprehension however being able to affect knowledge in a global sense. It is self-evident that dogmatism — whether rightly or wrongly so called — has value only insofar as the immutability of its axioms derives from that of principles, hence of truth.[17]

17. According to Kant, dogmatism is the "dogmatic process of pure reason, without prior critique of its capacity," or "a manner of philoso-phizing *(vernünfteln)* conveniently about things of which one understands nothing and of which no one in the world will ever understand anything." This brings us back, on the one hand, to the picture of the non-swimmer trying to get himself unaided out of the water and, on the other, to a confession of ignorance, to stupidity erected into universal law and mys-tique; what in fact is more irrational than this denial of intelligence in others — itself a perfect example of "dogmatism" and in any case convenient?

It is here — let us say in passing — that the hiatus between youth and mature age is situated; what youth has difficulty in understanding a priori — and even if it understands it in theory, the relevant reflexes generally are missing — is that things can in practice change their value according to unforeseen modes, and that it is the modalities which introduce the paradoxes and enigmas into existence, with their result of legitimate disappointments and exaggerated resentments.

But to return to empiricism: there is no worse confession of intellectual impotence than to boast concerning a line of thought because of its attachment to experiment and its disdain for principles and speculations.

*

* *

One of the most characteristic forms of denial of the Intellect is the prejudice which seeks to reduce the intelligence to the element of passion: without passion, it is said, there is no will to know, no effort, no knowledge. Now, intelligence is intelligence and passion is passion; the difference exists, or the two terms would not exist. There is no question but that every manifestation, be it macrocosmic or microcosmic, physical or mental, requires the cooperation of a dynamic element, but this has nothing whatever to do with the nature of intelligence; this latter remains virgin in relation to desire as long as desire does not impinge on the intellectual domain, that is to say, does not determine thought. The fact that the enunciation of a truth is necessarily accompanied by an act of will is entirely indifferent, since this act of will does not modify the truth but on the contrary arises by virtue of it; it simply forms a part of existence.

Essentially, man knows not by an act of will but as a result of perception: when an object impinges on our vision, it is not because we have had a desire to see it, but because our eye is sensitive to light rays. Instead of asserting that everything starts from passion, it could just as well be said that everything starts from knowledge, for there can be no passion for an object which is totally unknown. To claim that man has knowledge thanks only to love or hatred, as some have done, is to confuse an occasional cause — love or hatred — with an essential cause, which proves the absurdity of such theories.

Following the same line of thought, we would point out an abuse of language which feeds the confusion between intelligence and sentiment: it is currently called "pessimism" to observe that black is black — we speak figuratively — and "optimism" to observe that white is white, as if a perception, whether intellectual or physical, depended on our good pleasure; in reality, pessimism consists in taking white for black, while optimism makes the opposite mistake, which means that both alike belong to the sentimental order; it is quite illogical, therefore, to apply these terms to operations of the intelligence.

"Objectivity" is often discussed in our times, but it is readily reduced to a purely volitional or moral attitude, a kind of softness in the face of error or injustice, as if indignation could not be a criterion of "consciousness of the object," and so of objectivity. Serenity can, it is true, result from a higher point of view where disequilibriums are reabsorbed into the universal Equilibrium, and there is then nothing to refute, since phenomena appear in their ontological interdependence, and therefore in their necessity; but there is a false serenity which becomes the accomplice of evil, and proves only one thing, namely that the person concerned does not see that a disequilibrium is a disequilibrium: the man who mistakes a scorpion for a dragonfly remains calm, but it does not follow that his vision is objective. Christ's wrath proved, not a lack of objectivity of course, but the ignominy of its object.

*

* *

The universality and immutability of the Intellect and of Truth imply that there can be no "metaphysical problems special to our times"; the problems of our times are either the results of abnormal situations, or the fruits of accumulated errors, and it is these latter which must first be corrected before even raising the question of whether objectively possible solutions exist. When "our times" are spoken of, it is most often with a sort of fatalism which accepts them, even eagerly — and this quite conforms to the prejudice according to which an actual "state of affairs" takes precedence over the truth, or rather is identified with it — as if the present process of decline were some blind force of nature for which man was in no way responsible, and as if this something inevitable — or this character of fatality — implied a quasi-normative value or a "categorical imperative"; man poses as a victim when faced with the fruit of his sin, but without giving the latter its name, indeed quite the contrary. Thinking which is harnessed to temporal contingencies — or those of "life," which comes to the same thing — thereby loses all its validity; for validity lies in the quality of objectivity or of absoluteness, without which thought is only a monologue or an agitation in the void; if mathematical truths have not visibly changed since antiquity, there seems still less reason why metaphysical truths should change. Scarcely have we been asked to take a certain philosopher seriously when we are already being told not only that some other has "gone past" him, but also that the first has himself meanwhile "evolved"; and if there is a shortage of arguments for excusing the falsity of an opinion, consolation is sought in declaring that it constitutes a sample of "human effort" or a "contribution to culture," and so on, as if the aim of intelligence were not the discernment of truth.[18]

18. In this line of ideas mention should be made of the mania for mixing painters and novelists with metaphysics, for seeking imaginary depths or all kinds of bizarre qualities in people like Cézanne or

In reality, the *philosophia perennis,* actualized in the West, though on different levels, by Plato, Aristotle, Plotinus, the Fathers and the Scholastics, constitutes a definitive intellectual heritage, and the great problem of our times is not to replace them with something better — for this something could not exist according to the point of view in question here[19] — but to return to the sources, both around us and within us, and to examine all the data of contemporary life in the light of the one, timeless truth.

One of the things that men of today seem to fear most is to appear naive, whereas there is really nothing more naive than to attribute naivety to the ancient sages of the East and the West, whose teachings embrace implicitly, and broadly, everything of value to be found among the precautions and subtleties of modern thought; a man has to have very little imagination to believe, with the satisfaction of a schoolboy who is promoted, that he has at last discovered what hundreds and thousands of years of wisdom did not know, and that on the level of pure intelligence.[20] Before seeking to "surpass" any "scholasti-

Dostoyevsky; in spirituality, to be "an artist" is an entirely different thing, insofar as such an expression is admissible on this plane; it is to have an immediate vision of universal qualities in phenomena, and of "proportions" and "rhythms" in the transcendent order.

19. It is evident that some doctrines are more profound than others, but that is not the question here, for a difference of level has nothing to do with "progress," all the less so since such a difference is independent of temporal sequence. Aristotelianism is a kind of exteriorization of Platonism, that is to say of the doctrine represented by the line Pythagoras-Socrates-Plato-Plotinus. The Middle Ages showed at times an awareness of the superiority of Plato over Aristotle; it is thus that Saint Bonaventure attributes "wisdom" to the former and "science" to the latter.

20. For Heidegger, for instance, the question of Being "proved intractable in the investigations of Plato and Aristotle" and: "what was formerly wrenched out of phenomena in a supreme effort of thought, although in a fragmentary and groping *(in ersten Anläufen)* manner, has long since been rendered trivial" *(Sein und Zeit).* Now, it is a priori excluded that

cism," one should at least understand it! And if one understood it, one would hardly any longer try to surpass it in the quite exterior and provisional field of words.

When a philosophy is put forward as the answer to unresolved problems, by virtue of what principle are we to admit that this answer, hitherto never given, could suddenly arrive in the brain of some thinker? If some philosopher, with a completely ineffective prudence which only pushes back the bounds of the difficulty, claims to be making at least some advance towards the truth, by virtue of what are we to believe, firstly, that the thesis in question is really an advance, and secondly, that the truth placed ideally at the end of the road will ever be attained? For one of two things is true: either such a philosopher is the first to give a definitive answer, and then one would like to know by virtue of what quality a man can be the first to discover not a continent or gunpowder, but a fundamental truth of the principial order, which would imply that this man was in fact the first to be intelligent; or else it is the case that no philosopher can give a definitive answer, nor consequently know whether

---

Plato and Aristotle should have "discovered" their ontology by dint of "thinking"; they were, at most, the first in the Greek world to consider it useful to formulate an ontology in writing. Like all modern philosophers, Heidegger is far from being aware of the quite "indicative" and "provisional" role of "thinking" in metaphysics; and it is not surprising that this writer should, as a "thinker," misunderstand the normal function of all thought and conclude: "It is a matter of finding and following a way which allows one to arrive at the clarification of the fundamental question of ontology. As for knowing whether this way is the sole way, or a good way, this can only be decided subsequently" (ibid.). It is difficult to conceive a more anti-metaphysical attitude. There is always this same prejudice of subjecting the intellect, which is qualitative in essence, to the vicissitudes of quantity, or in other words of reducing every quality from an absolute to a relative level. It is the classical contradiction of philosophers: knowledge is decreed to be relative, but in the name of what is this decree issued?

such an answer is possible or not, and then the philosophy which "is moving towards a goal" is itself reduced to nothing. This can also be expressed as follows: if a certain thesis is capable of serving as an approximate and provisional indication of absolute truth, it is because the latter exists and one is aware of it, so that there is no need to resort to gropings; a thesis is true or it is not true, and if the said indication is true, it is because it is itself truth; error could not "indicate" anything whatsoever. A thesis which is regarded as remaining prudently aloof from the truth is not only no preparation for anything, but is obviously false in itself. If we must be content with "indications" — by way of working tools we are told — because the truth is inaccessible, then our conjectures are false by definition; it is absurd to present the inaccessibility of truth as being a truth, or to think that truth can be sought outside itself. Or again: if truth is inaccessible in principle, there is no explaining the existence of the concept or the word truth; if it has hitherto been inaccessible in fact, there is no reason to admit that it will ever be attained, and above all there is no possible explanation for this temporary inaccessibility. We could compare philosophical research to the vain efforts of an eye to see itself, as if the mystery of visibility were not revealed on the one hand by the nature of outward light and on the other by the intelligence. Another image which comes to mind is that of a kitten chasing its own tail, which is not a joke, but a rigorously adequate comparison. We do not deny that such and such a new thesis may represent, in relation to a preceding theory, a corrective movement in the direction of a partial truth, whence the illusion of a real progress; but such a tendency will in practice have merely the function of the positive phase in a pendular movement resulting from the initial contradiction inherent in the rationalist point of view. In other words, profane thinkers cannot fail to sterilize their acquired truths by new errors, and this proves precisely that an apprehension of the truth is possible only on the foundations, and within the framework, willed by God.[21]

*

*   *

To sum up our exposition and at the risk of repeating ourselves, we say that all anti-intellectual philosophy falls into this trap: it claims, for example, that there is only the subjective and the relative, without taking account of the fact that this is an assertion which, as such, is valid only on condition that it is itself neither subjective nor relative, for otherwise there would no longer be any difference between correct perception and illusion, or between truth and error. If "everything is true that is subjective," then Lapland is in France, provided we imagine it so; and if everything is relative — in a sense which excludes all reflection of absoluteness in the world — then the definition of relativity is equally relative, absolutely relative, and our defini-

---

21. What good, for example, is Schelling's correct view of intellectual contemplation and of the transcending of the subject-object relationship in the Absolute, since it is accompanied by the promise of a flat philosophical pseudo-religion mingled with a classical or academic aestheticism of the most banal style? The replacing of the Cartesian *Cogito ergo sum* by the formula of Maine de Biran: "I act, I will, I exist," or the *Sum cogitans* of Heidegger, and so on, is strictly a matter of taste, or of mental illusion; the starting point in all cases of this kind is at bottom merely an ignorance ignorant of itself. It may well be asked why thought or action are any better proof of our existence than some sensation or other; it is precisely the intelligence which shows us that many things exist without thinking, acting or willing, for once we see that stones exist, we have no need to invoke thought or action as proofs of our own existence, provided, of course, we admit that we are certain of the objective value of our vision. Now we are certain of it by virtue of the infallibility of the Intellect, and that is a subject which admits of no discussion, any more than does the question of knowing whether we are sane or mad. Philosophers readily found their systems on the absence of this certitude, which is however the *conditio sine qua non* of all knowledge, and even of all thought and all action.

tion has no meaning. Relativists of all kinds — the "existentialist" and "vitalist" defenders of the infra-rational — have then no excuse for their bad habits of thought.

Those who would dig a grave for the intelligence[22] do not escape this fatal contradiction: they reject intellectual discrimination as being "rationalism" and in favor of "existence" or of "life," without realizing that this rejection is not "existence" or "life" but a "rationalist" operation in its turn, hence something considered to be opposed to the idol "life" or "existence"; for if rationalism — or let us say intelligence — is opposed, as these philosophers believe, to fair and innocent "existence" — that of vipers and bombs among other things — then there is no means of either defending or accusing this existence, nor even of defining it in any way at all, since all thinking is supposed to "go outside" existence in order to place itself on the side of rationalism, as if one could cease to exist in order to think.

In reality, man — insofar as he is distinct from other creatures on earth — is intelligence; and intelligence — in its principle and its plenitude — is knowledge of the Absolute; the Absolute is the fundamental content of the intelligence and determines its nature and functions. What distinguishes man from animals is not knowledge of a tree, but the concept — whether explicit or implicit — of the Absolute; it is from this that the whole hierarchy of values is derived, and hence all notion of a homogeneous world. God is the "motionless mover" of every operation of the mind, even when man — reason — makes himself out to be the measure of God.

To say that man is the measure of all things is meaningless unless one starts from the idea that God is the measure of man, or that the Absolute is the measure of the relative, or again, that the universal Intellect is the measure of individual existence; nothing is fully human that is not

22. Kierkegaard, Nietzsche, Klages and others like them.

determined by the Divine, and therefore centered on it. Once man makes of himself a measure, while refusing to be measured in turn, or once he makes definitions while refusing to be defined by what transcends him and gives him all his meaning, all human reference points disappear; cut off from the Divine, the human collapses.

In our day, it is the machine which tends to become the measure of man, and thereby it becomes something like the measure of God, though of course in a diabolically illusory manner; for the most "advanced" minds it is in fact the machine, technics, experimental science, which will henceforth dictate to man his nature, and it is these which create the truth — as is shamelessly admitted — or rather what usurps its place in man's consciousness. It is difficult for man to fall lower, to realize a greater mental perversion, a more complete abandonment of himself, a more perfect betrayal of his intelligent and free personality: in the name of "science" and of "human genius" man consents to become the creation of what he has created and to forget what he is, to the point of expecting the answer to this from machines and from the blind forces of nature; he has waited until he is no longer anything and now claims to be his own creator. Swept away by a torrent, he glories in his incapacity to resist it.

And just as matter and machines are quantitative, so man too becomes quantitative: the human is henceforth the social. It is forgotten that man, by isolating himself, can cease to be social, whereas society, whatever it may do — and it is in fact incapable of acting of itself — can never cease to be human.

*
* *

The problem of intellectuality presents yet another aspect, this time in the religious field: there are those who criticize intellectual contemplation — always confused with ratiocination — for "willing" to penetrate the divine mysteries, as if it were not a contradiction in terms to attribute a "will" to pure intelligence, which is contemplation and nothing else. Those who formulate such objections admit a "metaphysical knowledge" only in mystical experience, in the grace which may arise gratuitously from the self-annihilation of the ascetic; but this amounts in practice and in the last analysis to reducing the distinction between truth and error to a question of will and grace.[23] If knowledge is nothing and if illuminating grace alone — conditioned by asceticism — has the power to give ontological certitudes together with the right to express them, of what use is this expression, since, if the intellect be inoperative, there is no faculty to understand it? There are those who would subordinate the intellectual element to the "existential," the "lived," doubtless in order to avoid mere "facility" and to maintain the supremacy of moral will and divine mystery over what are believed to be purely human speculations, but they forget that an affirmation is true, not because it has been formulated by someone who is considered to have experienced the highest degree of asceticism, but simply because it corresponds to reality; acceptance of an intelligible and communicable truth could not depend on more or less conjectural extrinsic criteria. An urge to debase and humanize the Intellect always betrays a certain instinct of self-preservation, a desire to safeguard something of the human in face of what is "inhuman" in truth. This explains the frequent paradox of a humility which makes itself the mouthpiece of a collective pride; a man will say for example that whoever has not received such and such sacramental and mystical graces could not spontaneously pronounce on the divine Truths, and, while recognizing his own individual incompetence, he will disparage all wisdom falling outside a particular religious framework. This is excusable

23. To affirm that grace is a "free gift" is to say that we do not know its causes, unless we are to attribute arbitrariness to God. The same remark is valid for the "gratuitousness" of Creation.

when it is done in the name of a dogma and without preoccupation with the content of the wisdom in question; but it is no longer excusable when taking part in discussions which, in this case, can only be question-begging. There is here an initial contradiction arising from the fact that the intelligence, which is reproached for not being an ascetico-mystical grace, is rejected, not by reference to such a grace but by reference to the intelligence itself; and what is to be said of unintelligence claiming kinship with sanctity in order to pretend that intelligence is valueless? In the same way, it is only too convenient and rather uncharitable to accuse of "pride" those who are more intelligent than oneself or to avenge oneself for failing to understand a superior intelligence by calling it childish, as is sometimes — with scant humility — done in respect to Hindu thought; it is true, however, that all this is characteristic of human nature. It is not a question of denying the existence of an intellectualist pride, that is to say of a will usurping the rights of pure intelligence and having the ambition to see what reason cannot attain, but the fact that such a defect exists does not authorize the banning of the vision of certain realities, in principle comprehensible, on the grounds that most men do not comprehend them.

Certainly, transcendent knowledge — provided it is real, that is to say "visionary" and not simply "dialectical" — is deepened by asceticism, for asceticism contributes in its own way to the transition from "knowing" to "being," from theory to realization, just as ascesis is in turn deepened by knowledge, where this latter is within the possibilities of the man; but when it is not so, ascesis has no power to produce gnosis — or rather to be the condition of its blossoming — for no discipline can modify the scope of the human receptacle, although it can doubtless produce, in the course of spiritual development, transmutations that seem miraculous. It is obviously absurd to evaluate some ascetic practice in terms of its possible fruits in respect of sacred knowledge, for that would oblige one to question the heroic qualities of many saints. And conversely, it is just as illogical to make this knowledge depend on conditions of will or morality which are comparatively external, for knowledge alone implies intrinsic certainty, that is to say it imposes itself by its very nature of intelligibility and self-evidence, and not by contingent conditions. This could also be expressed as follows: if knowledge is a grace, it is a free gift, and if it is freely given, it could not depend essentially on attitudes of will, otherwise it would be necessary to conclude that grace is their product; or again, if knowledge cannot depend, subjectively, on an extrinsic condition such as ascetic effort, truth in its turn cannot depend, objectively, on an extrinsic condition such as its attachment to a subjective phenomenon, namely the ascetic perfection of a particular individual. Moreover, if on the one hand it be admitted that ascesis is a preparation for grace — in the sense of a logical condition and not of an efficient cause — it must on the other hand be understood that metaphysical intellection, which is direct and therefore "concrete," implies a certain detachment with regard to the world and the "I," and demands a posteriori an ascesis conforming to its nature. And let us repeat here that intellection has absolutely nothing to do with mental "crutches" such as the "law of non-contradiction" or the "law of sufficient reason" and so on, although on the mental plane logic has its part to play, and although from another angle these laws translate aspects of the divine Wisdom.

Man can, in a certain sense,[24] will what God does not will; but he cannot in any sense know what God does not know. Vice always comes from the will, but error as such never comes from knowledge; hence there is in the intellect an

24. "In a certain sense" for, if it be true that God does not desire sin, there is, in the last analysis, nothing that takes place outside the divine Will. God "wills evil" insofar as the latter is a necessary element in the cosmic equilibrium; to cut off evil from the world would mean to abolish the world.

element of participation or union with God, a supernatural and not simply human element, and this marks in an eminently qualitative way a clear distinction between knowledge and will. To say that the intellect can "penetrate" the divine mysteries — and it can do so for the simple reason that it bears traces of them in its very substance — does not mean that it can "exhaust" them, for God is infinite, and the mirror is not the object it reflects, any more than the "Son" is the "Father." In reality, it is not the intellect which penetrates God, but God who penetrates the intellect; no one can choose God who has not been chosen by Him.

The Nature and Arguments of Faith

Faith is the conformity of the intelligence and the will to revealed truths. This conformity is either formal alone or else essential, in the sense that the object of faith is a dogmatic form and, behind this, an essence of Truth. Faith is belief when the volitive element predominates over the intellectual; it is knowledge or gnosis when the intellectual element predominates over the volitive. But there are also certitude and fervor, the latter being volitive and the former intellectual: fervor gives belief its spiritual quality; certitude is an intrinsic quality of gnosis. The term "faith" could not mean exclusively belief or fervor, nor exclusively knowledge or certitude; it cannot be said either that belief that it is all that is possible in the way of faith, or that knowledge is not faith at all.

In other words, faith, on whatever level it is envisaged, has an aspect of participation and an aspect of separation: of participation because its subject is intelligence which as such participates "vertically" in the Truth, and of separation because intelligence is limited "horizontally" by its plane of existence, which separates it from the divine Intellect. In the first respect faith is "certitude," whether its object compels acceptance through material or rational proofs, or whether it reveals its nature in pure intellection; in the second respect, faith is "obscurity" because the believing subject is existentially separated from the object of belief. Neither crude reason — that is, reason deprived

43

of suprarational illuminations due to our fall — nor a fortiori the body, can behold the celestial mysteries.

Intellection appears to the exoteric outlook to be an act of the reason wrongly claiming freedom from obscurity and falsely asserting independence with regard to Revelation. In reality, obscurity in intellective knowledge differs from obscurity in the reason by the fact that it is linked, not to intelligence itself, but to the ego insofar as it has not been transmuted by spiritual realization; intellective vision, in fact, does not imply a prior integration of our whole being in the Truth. As for Revelation, intellection lives by it, for it receives thence its whole formal armature; thus intellection cannot replace the objective, prophetic, lawgiving and traditional manifestation of the divine Intellect. One can neither conceive a Saint Augustine without the Gospel, nor a Shankaracharya without the Veda.[1]

This leads us to consider that there is a faith which can increase, just as there is one which is immutable: faith is immutable through the content and number of its dogmas, as also through the metaphysical immutability of the truth, or again, in the firmness of personal belief or in the incorruptibility of knowledge; as for the faith which may increase, it can be trust in the absolute veracity of Revelation, or fervent faithfulness to it; but, according to the point of view, this faith can also be the spiritual penetration of dogmas, namely gnosis.

Some people will doubtless point out that to use the word "faith" as a synonym for "gnosis" is to rob it of all meaning, since "seeing" is opposed to "believing," which is to say that faith requires both obscurity of understanding and the merit of free adherence: but this distinction, which is legitimate on its own level, where it reflects a real situation, involves the disadvantage of limiting scriptural terminology

---

1. It is this a priori — and not a posteriori — dependence of intellection with regard to Revelation which is so well expressed by Saint Anselm's saying *Credo ut intelligam.*

to the exoteric point of view; this latter point of view cannot determine the scope of the divine Word, although, inversely, the divine Word is crystallized with a view to the necessities of exoterism, whence its universality. Faith, as we have said, is the adherence of the intelligence to Revelation; now, if exoterism reduces intelligence to reason alone, while replacing the intellect — the supra-rational nature of which it cannot conceive — by grace, which it sees as the sole supernatural element, this restriction, though opportune, cannot change the nature of things nor abolish the intellective faculty where it exists; the concept of "faith" thus necessarily keeps its inner limitlessness and its polyvalence, for there can be no question, in a religious civilization, of denying faith to those whose intelligence transcends the ordinary limits of human understanding.

The matter could also be expressed in this way: exoterism is not, and cannot be, aware of the existence of an intellective "paracletic" faculty, but on the other hand it cannot admit that intelligence should, by its own nature, be contrary to faith. Now not to exclude reason from the realm of faith is implicitly not to exclude the total intelligence, for the limiting of intelligence to reason alone is merely accidental; the total character of faith thus involves an implicit acceptance of the intellect. What matters here is not that "faith" is distinct from "science," but that it is the total adherence of the intelligence as such to transcendent Truth. The concept of faith is traditional, and the intellect exists; consequently, this concept must have, besides its literal and as it were collective meaning, the quality of a pure symbol; it must remain valid at all possible levels.

Now if faith, being an adherence of the intelligence, is necessarily identical in its center with knowledge (to say that the blessed no longer have faith means that they have knowledge where ordinary mortals have belief), it is obvious that knowledge is not identical with faith in the general sense of this term, for the lesser can symbolize the greater but not the converse; the existence in the scriptures of the word "gnosis" must moreover have some a sufficient reason. However that may be, the human groups which lie outside the field of the Semitic dogmatisms have no reason to include — or to envelop — the universal concept of knowledge in the particular concept of faith: adherence to a Revelation has not everywhere the same character of merit that it possesses among Westerners, including here Moslems, and the question of freedom of adherence does not arise everywhere as it does in the case of the Western religions. We do not think we are going too far in saying that the necessity for a dogmatic faith answers to a collective tendency to deny the supernatural in accordance with a mentality which is more passional than contemplative and thereby riveted to "bare facts," whence a philosophy which makes deductions from the sensory to the Universal, instead of starting from the latter in order to understand the former; it is not a question here of passion as such, which is a general human fact, but of its intrusion into the field of the intelligence. In the East, except among Moslems, there are no dogmas properly speaking, for ideas are considered there as points of departure which are more or less provisional — although absolute on their respective planes — so that what is true on a given plane ceases to be so on another; in these conditions, faith could not be affectively centered on a credo, or in other words, conviction is less the complement of a doubt than a quasi-existential axiom. For a Hindu the psychological equivalent of the Judaeo-Christian faith will above all be fervent attachment *(shraddhā)* to a given path *(mārga)*, to a master *(guru)*, to a given aspect of the Divine *(ishta);* this kind of faith, which is a "manner of being" rather than a "belief," is indeed indispensable to all spiritual life, Western as well as Eastern. In the *jnāna-mārga*, it is ultimately necessary to go beyond this fervor, for it too is only illusion; in a general way, a Hindu will not bring knowledge into relationship with faith, since for him gnosis does not have to be fitted into a traditional framework exoteric in form.

*

*   *

Apart from the imponderable factors of grace, it is by virtue of its proofs that dogmatic faith compels acceptance. Such proofs may lie either in the field of facts, or in that of ideas; in the first case, proof lies in miracles or prophecy, and in the second, in a sort of intellectual self-evidence. These two kinds of proof never exclude one another, but one of them will be predominant: when it is miracle that predominates — the supernatural fact, the intervention of the Celestial in the terrestrial — the intellectual side of faith will appear as obscure, it will be essentially "mystery"; when it is evidence — the metaphysical idea, the irresistible force of Truth — which predominates then the existential side of faith, the sacred facts, will appear as relatively secondary, being subordinate to the Truth which determines them in advance and prevents them from becoming the culminating points of a religious "mythology." In other words, one faith is distinguished from another, not only by its content, but also by its subjective structure depending on whether it is centered on the persuasive force of the sacred fact or on that of the revealed idea; herein lies the fundamental difference between the Christian and Islamic perspectives. Every religion comprises both outward proofs and inward evidences; the difference which we are speaking about is a question of emphasis and predominance, not of exclusive principle.

The element miracle and the element truth are as it were the two poles of Revelation: grace is wrought by the miracle, while intellectual certitude is engendered by the truth; grace is a kind of passive intellection, while intellection is an active or participative grace. We could also say this: Revelation and intellection are the poles of faith, one being objective and macrocosmic, the other subjective and microcosmic: but Revelation also has an aspect of intellection, and intellection for its part an aspect of Revelation.

Indeed, Revelation is as it were the intellection — or the intellect — of the collectivity, in the sense that it compensates for the absence of intellectual intuition, not in an individual, but in a human collectivity subject to given conditions. By contrast, intellectual intuition is as it were Revelation within the individual; that is to say, that which is Revelation with regard to "a humanity"[2] will be, analogously, intellection for an individual, and conversely. If every man possessed intellect, not merely in a fragmentary or virtual state, but as a fully developed faculty, there would be no Revelations, since total intellection would be a natural thing; but as it has not been like this since the end of the Golden Age, Revelation is not only necessary but even normative in respect to individual intellection, or rather in respect to its formal expression. No intellectuality is possible outside the language of Revelation, a scriptural or oral tradition, although intellection can occur, as an isolated miracle, wherever the intellective faculty exists; but an intellection outside tradition will have neither authority nor efficacy. Intellection has need of occasional causes in order to become fully aware of itself and be exercised unfettered; therefore in milieus that are practically speaking deprived of Revelation — or forgetful of the sapiential significances of the revealed Word — intellectuality exists in general only in a latent state; even where it is still affirmed despite everything, perceived truths are made inoperative by their too fragmentary character and by the mental chaos which surrounds them. Revelation is for the intellect like a principle of actualization, expression and control; the revealed "letter" is in practice indispensable in intellectual life, as we have already said.

2. Every Revelation is addressed, in principle, to man and so to humanity as a whole; but in fact, it concerns only "one humanity," because of the segmentation of humankind and the mental incompatibilities which result from it; this partial humanity takes the place of the totality of humankind.

Allusion was made above to the respective positions of Christianity and Islam: the great extrinsic arguments of Christian faith are, in time, the prophecies, and in space, the miracles; the coming of Christ is itself the miracle par excellence. By contrast, the arguments of Moslem faith are, first of all the evidence[3] of the transcendent and creating Unity and secondly the normative and universal character of the unitary Revelation; this Revelation is normative because it rests on the natural properties of things with a realism that puts everything in its place and avoids confusing realms and levels; and it is universal because it seeks to teach only what has been taught for all time. "In space," it might be said, the argument of Islam is its character of being a norm, which in its way embraces all the religions, since it retraces their essential positions, and "in time" the argument is the continuity or invariability of the Message, that is to say the fact that every preceding Message, from Adam to Jesus, is none other than submission *(islām)* to the One *(Allāh)*. "In space," Islam appears thus as a polyvalent pattern; "in time," it presents itself as a restoration of what has been before it, since the creation of man. Let us note that altogether analogous formulations could be made, *mutatis mutandis,* taking Christian gnosis as the starting point: the mystery of the Word in fact embraces every possible Revelation, every truth is necessarily manifested in terms of Christ and on His model; this perspective is nonetheless more veiled than the corresponding perspective in Islam by reason of the predominance of historical fact; it is true that Muhammad, too, appeared as such a fact, but the unitary perspective of Islam comprises an extrinsically "leveling" character which greatly diminishes the terrestrial unique-

3. The French word *évidence* is often translated as "evidence" in this and related passages; but it is necessary to have in mind that in such contexts the word comprises the two meanings of "evidentness" (or self-evidence) and "testimony" (Translator's note).

ness of the Prophet.[4] The "Unification" *(tawhīd)* contained in Islam is accompanied by a "leveling" in time and space; as Unity determines and absorbs everything, no fact can be "absolutely unique."

We could also say that for Islam God — intrinsic Reality and universal Cause — "has always been" God; and the intelligence — principle and organ of faith — "has always been" the intelligence; in other words, the Truth — the reflection of God in the intelligence, or the latter's participation in God — "has always been" the Truth, so that no religion can be "new." It is this idea or this sentiment which gives the Moslem his quasi-organic conviction of the sureness of his religion's foundations, while the analogous sentiment for the Christian is based on the divine character of Christ, as well as on the fulgurant intelligibility of His work of redemption. In Christianity, everything depends on recognizing the efficacy of the divine "lifeline of salvation," attaching oneself to it with all one's being and despite the world; in Islam, everything depends on opening one's eyes to the unitary light and following it everywhere: in the accidental, where it puts everything in its place, and in the essential, where it transforms and liberates. The difference as regards original sin, is that Christianity identifies man with his will, whence the absolute and hereditary character of Adam's fall, whereas Islam identifies man with his mind

4. Thus the attestation that "Muhammad is the Messenger of God" *(Muḥammadun Rasūlu 'Llāh)* embraces, according to Moslem theology, the attestation of all the Messengers; on the other hand, however, the fact that the Prophet is the last of the line and the "Seal of Prophecy" *(Khātam an-nubuwwah)* introduces into Islam something of that "uniqueness of manifestation" which is characteristic of Christianity, and which must be found in every religion to some degree or other, religion having by definition a "central" character. If Islam attenuates and neutralizes the absoluteness of the Prophet by accepting a series of preceding and equivalent prophets, the same is true and even more so of the avataric doctrine in Hindusim and Buddhism, which admits a plurality or even a multitude of "incarnations."

— the intelligence which raises man above the animal —
whence the relative nature of the fall; "infidelity" comes
from the intelligence being submerged by the passions, and
it is the predisposition to this decadence which is hereditary, and not the state of submersion. Christianity grasps the
fall in its cause, which belongs to the will, Adam having
betrayed his intelligence by his corruptible will, whence the
crucial function, in this perspective, of sacrifice. Islam, by
contrast, considers the fall only in its effects — the passions,
which may exist or not exist — putting the accent on the
incorruptibility of intelligence as such: the latter, in fact,
cannot be corrupted in its true nature, but it can be buried
beneath the passions, which come of a corrupted will; now
unitary faith canalizes and neutralizes the passions "from
without" by the Law *(shari'ah)*, and dissolves them "from
within" by the Path *(tariqah)* or by Virtue *(ihsān)*, which
implies detachment with regard to the (idolatrous)
"associations" of this world.[5]

5. The fact that Islam "skirts around" the "original sin" aspect, basing
itself on that which defines man and which thus gives him a "relatively
absolute" character, namely intelligence or responsibility — this fact
appears clearly in a rite such as ablution; the latter envisages the original
stain, not in its cause, since Islam does not take this into consideration,
but in its effects, the physical impurities of fallen man *(bashar);* the
original stain is thus neutralized through the contact with God, but its
definitive elimination belongs to knowledge *(ma'rifah)*. This neutraliza-
tion is brought about through the medium of water — sometimes
through sand or a stone — because the elements, being simple, are
incorruptible; the rite restores to them, for the time being, their Edenic
and purifying reality. Christianity, which takes the original stain as being
essential in man since he is considered in his volitive nature — the
intelligence then becoming secondary, except in gnosis where it is an
emanation of the Word — Christianity, we say, takes sin from the point of
view of its intentionality, thus in its cause and in its center, and does so
through the medium of confession, which in principle purifies the soul
definitively. If we may speak without euphemism, but also without intend-
ing censure, we would add that a certain kind of Christian mysticism is
not far removed from seeing in unintelligence, ugliness and uncleanness

It should be noted in this connection that Islam combines the Mosaic law of retaliation with the charity of Christ, the latter concerning more particularly what is immortal in man, and the former the earthly collectivity. Islam, like Judaism, recognizes the divine element in the "law of the jungle": this law of the strongest is the expression of the biological equilibrium of species, hence of the economy of natural life; and as man incontestably has an aspect of animality since he has a body and reproduces himself, multiplying and eventually degenerating, the "law of the jungle" — or rather "natural selection" — necessarily governs him to some extent, and especially in his collective life;[6] to deny this would be to confuse the earth with Heaven and to attribute to men the status of angels. But this law, precisely because it reflects on its own level the nature of things and exists only by reason of the collectivity, could not by itself obstruct the spirituality of the individual,[7] and all the less so since tradition always leaves doors open for certain vocational liberties — hermits, pilgrims and monks live almost outside society — and since the quality of *homo sapiens* or of "rational animal" combined with the virtue of charity can and should compensate the rigors of biological

something like spiritual values, evidently connected with love, suffering, inner purity, heroic humiliation; but since this way of seeing things is clearly not exclusive, it is not surprising that other perspectives, for example that of Islam, should adopt a different point of view and deliberately lay stress on intelligence and beauty, as also on cleanliness, in this case ritual cleanliness; this point of view cannot fail to be affirmed also in the climate of Christianity.

6. It may be observed that there are certain tribes of noble character who live partly by plunder and people feel indignant at this moral contradiction, as if these tribes were alone in appropriating other people's goods, which they do moreover not without some generosity. Brigandage is the imperialism of nomads, just as imperialism is the brigandage of large nations.

7. This is shown for example in the teaching of the *Bhagavad Gītā*, which is contemplative and warlike at the same time, and above all in the case of sainted monarchs.

fatality. As for the apparent injustices in the latter, it must not be forgotten that in a world still traditional[8] though already chaotic, spiritual superiority definitively prevails over simple force, so that the law of "vital economy" is compensated by a law of the spirit.[9]

To sum up, the Islamic — or more precisely the Sufi — Path presents itself as a reduction of diversity to Unity or of form to Essence, just as, on an outward plane, Islam appears as the coordination of a chaos around a center or as the transmutation of a disordered movement into a rhythm. Christianity, for its part, is essentially the entry — or the descent — of the Principle into the cosmos, the Divine into the human, with a view to deification, namely the reintegra-

8. We say "in a world still traditional," an all-important reservation, because in the modern world the equilibrium between the "normal forces" has been broken, so that the aggressive use of force no longer retains any aspect of relative legitimacy; the "jungle," the creation of God, is replaced by the machine, the creation of man; the "tacit understanding" between the jungle and the spirit is abolished in favor of an iconoclastic and hypocritical materialism, which seeks to justify itself by a humanitarian, but worldly and anti-spiritual idealism. From another standpoint, it is obvious that the law of the strongest, which is always relative and conditional, cannot provide the least excuse for baseness, perfidious lying and cowardly treachery; the jungle offers no examples of these specifically human possibilities.

9. The victory of Judaeo-Christian monotheism over the Greco-Roman and barbarian worlds, and that of Buddhism and Islam over the Mongols, not forgetting the spiritual resistance of Hinduism against the Moslem potentates, prove that the victors "according-to-this-world" always end either by being absorbed, or by being neutralized, as the case may be, by forces which are not "of-this-world." In the case of the opposition between Hinduism and Islam, the latter appeared only in its quality of conquering power, at least to the extent that Hinduism still possessed sufficient vitality, and apart from the spiritual radiation of the Sufis with respect to the Vishnuites. What is disconcerting from the Christian point of view in the person of Muhammad, is that the Prophet incarnates at one and the same time both the law of the spirit and that of the jungle; we could say the same of the Jewish Prophets, but in this case the Christian point of view would hold God responsible for the jungle, which from the Moslem angle would obviously seem inconsequential.

tion of the human into the Divine. The Christian mystery is incarnation and crucifixion: sanctity is like unto the incarnation of the Word in the body of the Virgin, who prefigures the soul in the state of grace; it is the "Christ liveth in me" of Saint Paul. But the ego is crucified, it expiates the darkness of the world, therefore the injunction to "resist not evil" (Matt. 5:39); this crucifixion is death to sin — to idolatrous desire[10] — and the birth of God within us. And this is important: whereas Islam places itself at a viewpoint according to which the world is in God in such a way that man is never cut off from God by a quasi-existential disgrace, the link being in the nature of things and not in some condition which may or may not be, Christianity, for its part, on the contrary envisages the cosmic drama from the angle of the "moral" fissure between God and man — an "infinite" fissure — so that the repairing Intermediary is everything. But there can be no watertight partitions between the different rhythms of the Spirit; the forms which Truth may assume are so many mirrors reflecting one another.

*

* *

10. Crucifixion also symbolizes the oppression of the Intellect by the passions: it is God in us who is martyred by our downfall. Let us recall in this connection that Christ, being the wisdom of the Father — or the "consciousness" of the divine Being — represents the Intellect in the three respects of the metacosmic, the macrocosmic and the microcosmic: the pure Intellect, which enlightens man, is a "Christic" mode just as is the universal Intellect which enlightens and sustains the world, and as is a fortiori the divine Intellect, which is the intrinsic Light of God; the macrocosmic and the microcosmic rays are "created" and "uncreate" at one and the same time, just as Christ is "true man and true God." The perspective of gnosis is centered on the Intellect: "God is Light," says the Gospel and "I am the light of the world"; "the light shineth in darkness"; "this is life eternal, that they might know thee."

According to Ibn Hanbal, any man who maintains that the whole of faith is created is an infidel; the uncreate element in faith reappears in the gnosis of Christianity, and also, though in objective or "separative" mode, in grace as understood by the Orthodox. For the Salimiyah — a school founded by the Sufi Sahl At-Tustari — wisdom is identical with faith: "God is Faith," that is to say Wisdom or Intellect; the perfection of faith — union — consists in becoming conscious of the divine "I," a perspective which rejoins that of the Vedantists. In the same order of ideas, but on a more external plane, certain Moslem theologians do not hesitate to assert that faith is valid only on condition that its intellectual proofs are known,[11] which shows that faith here has its

11. We might speak here of "rational proofs," but it is necessary to take account of the following: just as, in Catholic theology, the intelligence is "accidentally" the reason owing to a collective situation, so too evidence, in Moslem theology, is "accidentally" rational owing to the very plane of exoterism. According to Abu Abdallah As-Sanusi (who is not to be confused with the much later founder of the Sanusi brotherhood), "intellectual judgement operates essentially according to three modes, in conformity with its objects: the necessary, the impossible and the possible. The necessary is that of which the absence is inconceivable; the impossible is that of which the existence cannot be conceived; the possible is that which, according even to natural intelligence, may either be or not be. Now every man subject to the duty of faith (that is to say every human being who has attained the age of reason) also has the duty, according to the divine Law, of knowing what must be affirmed on the subject and finally what (being possible without being necessary) can be said of God (in such or such a respect)" (*Aqīdat ahl at-tawḥīd aṣ-ṣughrā*, "Little Catechism"). A later authority, Muhammad Al-Fudali, expresses himself thus: "Every Moslem must know fifty dogmas, each with its general and (even) particular proofs; according to authoritative opinion, the general proof is enough. When, for example, someone asks: What is the proof of the reality (the 'existence,' *wujūd*) of God? The answer will be: creatures. Do these latter prove the reality of God by their contingence or by their becoming in time? Now if the man who is questioned does not indicate this distinction but is content with the reference to creatures, his proof will be general, which is enough from the point of view of the Law. Faith according to the authority (of another) is to accept the fifty dogmas

roots in evidence,[12] in the inward pole, not in the historical fact. However, the "obscurity" of faith is still maintained here by the fact that it is a priori a matter of exoterism: "No imagination attains it, no reason grasps it, no creature resembles it," says the famous theological treatise of Ahmad At-Tahawi, and: "He who desires to know what is closed to him and whose reason is not satisfied with a state of resignation is, by his very desire, separated from union with God, from pure knowledge and true faith; he oscillates between infidelity and faith. . . ."[13] This is not a denial of

without knowing their general and particular proofs. Some (the Asharites) have held the opinion that faith according to authority (alone) discloses a (legally) insufficient knowledge of the (revealed) faith, for example, Ibn Al-'Arabi (the jurist, not the Sufi) and As-Sanusi (the theologian); in their view, faith according to authority (alone) amounts to infidelity *(kufr)*" *(Kifāyat al-awwāmmi fīmā yajibu 'alayhim min 'ilm al-kalām,* "Sufficient Catechism"). Further on in the same treatise we find the following declaration: "By understanding (of the proofs of God) the (sane-minded) Moslem leaves the bonds of the faith by authority; he who has only this (blind) faith falls into everlasting fire, according to the doctrine of Ibn Al-'Arabi and of As-Sanusi." It is not the divergence of view on the subject of hell which matters to us here (the rigorists are right about the cases where ignorance of canonical proofs is a matter of voluntary negligence due to indifference and pride), but what is important is the unanimous disapproval of blind faith. Nevertheless, this faith by authority *(īmān al-muqallid)* is considered sufficient for the simple by the Hanafite and Malikite theologians.

12. The intellectual — and thereby the rational — foundation of Islam results in the average Moslem having a curious tendency to believe that non-Moslems either know that Islam is the truth and reject it out of pure obstinacy, or else are simply ignorant of it and can be converted by elementary explanations; that anyone should be able to oppose Islam with a good conscience quite exceeds the Moslem's power of imagination, precisely because Islam coincides in his mind with the irresistible logic of things. Within the same order of ideas, it is significant that some Moslem theologians consider that Christianity corresponds to sentiment and Islam to reason.

13. In the same way Abu Zayd Al-Qayrawani teaches in his *Risālah:* "Among these obligations is faith with the heart, and testimony with the tongue, concerning the truth that God is a unique Divinity: there is no

gnosis, for a distinction must be made between "understanding" what the Intellect reveals and "wishing to understand" what it does not reveal. The whole distinction here is in the gap between "understanding" and "willing" or, provided a 'sense of proportion is preserved, between an attitude that is "prophetic" and one that is "promethean"; one can be forbidden, not indeed to know, but to seek to discover by processes of reasoning what reason is incapable of attaining by its own means. The rights of intellection remain imprescriptible: a *ḥadīth* in fact teaches that "God has created nothing better than the intelligence, nothing more perfect, nothing more beautiful; the blessings that God grants are due to it (since it determines freedom of choice); understanding comes from it, and the wrath of God strikes him who despises it."[14]

Christianity puts the emphasis on grace without however excluding the help of reason, since the latter exists, whereas for Islam reason has a position necessarily connected with faith and in its way prefigures the intellect. For Christianity, the blessed in Heaven have faith no longer, since they have the beatific vision: believing is essentially accepting without

divinity outside Him; He has no like, no equal, no son, no father, no companion, no associate; He has neither beginning nor ending; the essence of His qualities escapes the description of men; human reflections cannot contain Him. Those who reflect derive a teaching from His signs (*āyāt*, the symbols of nature); but they cannot penetrate His Essence, nor understand anything of His Knowledge beyond what He permits."

14. "Faith and intelligence are brothers; God does not accept one of them without the other." This saying of Sayyidna Ali is characteristic of the perspective in question, which puts the emphasis on the intellective element of faith rather than its volitive element. Abu Bakr said: When I see a thing I see God before it. Omar replied: When I see a thing, I see God behind it. Othman said: When I see a thing, I see God in it. And Ali: When I see a thing, I see God." This tale refers again to the intellective side of faith, and the degree expressed by Sayyidna Ali corresponds to the realization of gnosis; the other points of view indicate the different intellectual junctions between the relative and the Absolute, or the various possible stages of thought and intuition.

seeing. Islam, while clearly admitting this definition — but in the sense of an earthly accidentality — insists rather on the content of faith and on our relationship with it: since neither this content, nor our union with this content ceases in the hereafter — quite the contrary — faith is common to those who dwell on earth and in Heaven. Here below it is "acceptance" and "conviction," and it increases or diminishes, not as regards its content but solely from the point of view of certitude; acceptance is dogmatic and static; conviction is spiritual and dynamic, it is not subject to any religious restriction. "There is but one (sole) faith: the faithful are equal in principle (through the acceptance of the truth); pre-eminence among them depends only on sincerity (of conviction) and (consequently) on mortification of the passions" (At-Tahawi). The word "sincerity" *(ikhlāṣ)* here means the tendency towards the most inward and purest truth *(ḥaqīqah);* the opposite of this sincerity is hypocrisy *(nifāq).* Just as sincerity is synonymous with intellectual and mystical profundity, so is hypocrisy synonymous with superficiality and lukewarmness, and that is why a man is called a hypocrite *(munāfiq)* who professes an opinion which indirectly infringes the doctrine of Unity; in other words, the hypocrite is the man who is morally or intellectually "inconsistent," sincerity being the sense of consistency, but in depth.

Moslem faith embraces in its own way what Christianity calls the theological virtues,[15] as also virtue in action, for acts of virtue are then being connected with faith in the sense that they increase it — in respect of conviction or sincerity, not in respect of dogmatic acceptance — while

15. Faith, hope and charity. Faith has for its subject primarily intelligence and secondarily the will: it concerns God insofar as He is the author of grace (here below) and of glory (in the hereafter). Hope and charity have the will as subject: hope is concerned with God insofar as He is our beatitude, and charity is concerned with Him insofar as He is perfect and lovable in Himself.

acts of disobedience diminish it.[16] There is no faith *(īmān)* without submission (religious submission, *islām)* — says Abu Hanifah — and no submission without faith." According to a *ḥadīth,* "the most excellent faith is to love him who loves God, to hate him who hates God,[17] to use the tongue ceaselessly in repeating the Name of God, to treat men as you would wish them to treat you and to reject for others what you would reject for yourselves." Now what makes faith most excellent is virtue (spiritual virtue, *iḥsān):* it is thanks to virtue that faith results in the "knowing" which is "being," at the "Oneness (or indivisibility) of Reality" *(waḥdat al-Wujūd).*

The fact that a religious proof seems to be addressed a priori to reason does not mean that it is therefore purely rational, or even rationalist, which is to say that its conclusion has no transcendent factor to guarantee it. The canonical argument, if it is addressed in the first place to reason, since it must take account of all degrees of understanding, is nonetheless guaranteed in its intrinsic truth by two properly "supernatural" factors, namely the Revelation which authenticates it, and the intellection from which it proceeds; these two factors are universal and not individual,

16. "It is necessary to believe that faith consists in testimony by word, in purity of heart and in actions of the organs (of sensation and of action); that it increases or diminishes in proportion to works, for they are capable of impoverishing or enriching it; that oral testimony of faith is perfect only when it is accompanied by acts; that every word and every action are of value only through their intention; that words, acts and intentions are of value only if they conform to traditional practice" *(sunnah,* teaching and example of the Prophet) (The *Risālah* of Al-Qayrawani).

17. In the sense — which is moreover the Gospel sense — of a "lesser charity" or a "conditional charity." Charity imposes no obligation to love error or vice; one must love men as such but not insofar as they are bad, that is to say insofar as they hate God. The Gospel demands the "hating of parents" with a view to loving God alone, although, in another respect, it clearly requires that they should be included in love of the neighbor by reason of the love God has for man.

the first in an objective manner in relation to the human microcosm, and the second in a subjective or inward manner in relation to the dogma, which comes from above. Profane philosophy is ignorant not only of the value of truth and universality in Revelation, but also of the transcendence of the pure Intellect;[18] it entails therefore no guarantee of truth on any level, for the quite human faculty which reason is, insofar as it is cut off from the Absolute, is readily mistaken even on the level of the relative. The efficacy of reasoning is essentially conditional.

The traditional proofs of dogmas are irrefutable within the framework of the mentality to which they are addressed; but they lose their sufficient reason, either entirely or partially, outside this mentality and the dogmatic formulations which correspond to it. It should be noted that a collective mentality does not always coincide with an ethnic group,[19] but that it depends also on certain psychological and spiritual conditions which may occur in the most diverse races having no apparent link between them; it is these psychological conditions — whatever their causes — which deter-

18. For example, the Cartesian *Cogito* is neither conformable to Revelation, nor the consequence of a direct intellection: it has no scriptural basis, since according to Scripture the foundation of existence is Being and not some experience or other; and it lacks inspiration, since direct intellective perception excludes a purely empirical process of reasoning. When Locke says *Nihil est in intellectu quod non prius fuerit in sensu,* the statement is false in the same two respects; firstly, Scripture affirms that the intellect derives from God and not from the body — for man, "made in the image of God," is distinguished from animals by the intelligence not by the senses — and secondly, the intellect conceives of realities which it does not discern a priori in the world, though it may seek their traces a posteriori in sensory perceptions.

19. The mental conditioning of Christianity or of Islam is much less ethnical than that of Judaism or of Confucianism, although the racial heritage no doubt never quite disappears; Europe has been "Judaized" by Christianity just as part of Asia has been "Arabized" by Islam, but these racial influences were possible only in function of psychological conditions far more generalized.

mine the "mental style" of a human group. This style is characterized, among other things, by some particular need for causality; also, the traditional dialectic is addressed not to the problems of an individual, but to the natural mentality of a collectivity, that is to say to a need for causal explanations which will be "acceptable to God" because it is "natural" and not arbitrary.

When we affirm that a proof of God is intrinsically irrefutable, we take no account, of course, of its apparent vulnerability, for it is clear that an artificial process of reasoning can contradict anything; but in this we are not interested in the least, any more than in the physical possibility of throwing a sacred book into the fire. There are three essential points which must never be lost sight of: firstly, that a truth is true, not because it can be demonstrated, but because it corresponds to a reality; secondly, that there is no possible demonstration which can satisfy every need of causality, given the fact that such need can be artificial; thirdly, that someone who will not be satisfied by a doctrinal demonstration can always claim that some truth — which for him will be a hypothesis — has not been demonstrated, or that it is false in itself, and so on. But every demonstration of a truth is in principle accessible to the man who knows this truth in a direct way, even if the dialectical contingencies belong to a system of thought other than his own.

*
* *

An example of the relative or conditional character of canonical proofs is the following text of Fudali: "God makes no use of an instrument in any activity. He is the Independent One *(Ghaniy)* in the absolute sense. The proof (of the divine Oneness) shows moreover that there is nothing outside the divine which can be really causative, for example the burning of fire . . . it is rather God who creates the burning in the object seized by the fire, even on each particular occasion. . . . He then who believes that it is the fire which causes the burning by virtue of its nature is an infidel (because he denies the uniqueness of the divine Cause by associating another cause with it). . . . And he who believes that the fire causes the burning by virtue of a particular force which God created in it, is astray and a hypocrite,[20] since he has not grasped the proper meaning of the doctrine of the Oneness of God." We have here a striking example of the spirit of alternatives characteristic of the Semitic and Western mentalities: in order to be able to affirm one essential aspect of truth, other aspects must be denied, although they would in no way derogate from the principle to be demonstrated. The Islamic theory of causative Oneness is entirely right in its positive content, but its theological formulation would be unacceptable to a Christian or a Hindu: to the former because his religion, based on the Trinity, has no need to insist on the causative Oneness, quite the contrary, and to the latter because the Western spirit of rigorous alternatives does not affect him. But the pure Semite must always guard against the danger of divinizing natural forces and thereby excluding ontological Unity.

Another example: "The fourth quality which of necessity pertains to God (God being, firstly real, secondly without origin, thirdly without end) is otherness in relation to temporal (created) things. . . . If God resembled a temporal thing in some particular point, He Himself would also have to be as temporal as that thing: for what is said about one of two things which coincide in kind is valid also for the other. . . . Since the temporal condition is denied for God, His otherness in relation to temporal things is affirmed. Consequently, there is no similitude, in any point, between

20. Let us recall that "hypocrisy" is synonymous with superficiality and is the opposite of "sincerity"; the attestation of Unity *(lā ilāha illā 'Llāh)* is deemed to oblige the "sincere" believer *(mukhlis)* to see things in the light of Unity.

God and temporal things. This is the general proof which it is a religious duty for every Moslem to know" (Fudali). Here again the spirit of alternatives appears distinctly: the idea that God as such, as Essence, is absolutely other than the world, here excludes the idea — which is nonetheless just as true, though independent of the unitary perspective — that things can, or even must, resemble God in respect of His Qualities, for it would otherwise be impossible to affirm, as does the Koran, that "God is the Light of the Heavens and of the earth"; a Hindu would even go so far as to say that visible light "is" — on a given level of manifestation — the divine Light. Of course, the canonical proofs of Islam are all that they ought to be, since they are addressed to a particular collective mentality; of necessity they are so formulated as to avoid such errors as are possible given the mentality under consideration. The metaphysician, for his part, will easily find the complementary and corrective aspects of the proofs in question, basing himself on the very formulations of the Koran; the sacred texts are never fundamentally at the mercy of mental contingencies, for being divine they are of necessity universal.

It cannot escape the theologians that the very existence of symbolism — which is by definition based on real analogies between the divine and cosmic orders — contradicts the exclusive aspect of the proof quoted; their reply to this objection would be that physical luminosity is of a totally different nature from divine Light; this suffices for the simple but it resolves nothing, since the terminology itself proves that there is analogy, hence "relative identity." To say that God is Light, but that light in no way resembles God is pure and simple contradiction; however, it can be said that divine Light differs absolutely from created light, whereas created light resembles divine Light, an elliptical formula which logically appears absurd, but which contains a doctrine all the more profound. In any case, the use of one and the same word to designate both a created quality and an uncreated quality proves that there is not a total difference in every respect; it might perhaps be possible to do justice to all shades of meaning by using a negative expression and saying that if the sun is luminous, God will be "non-dark," a subtlety which is far from useless for him who understands it. Dialectical precautions always become necessary where the level of understanding is too rational; if one were speaking to men of the Golden Age, one could say without hesitation that "the light is God," one could even "worship the sun," or at least seem to do so.

But let us now consider an example drawn from Christianity: "If any man says that finite things, be they corporal or spiritual, or at any rate spiritual, have emanated from the divine Substance, or that the divine Essence, by its manifestations or evolutions, becomes all things, or finally that God is the universal and undefined Being who, in determining Himself, constitutes the totality of things which are divided into genders, species or individuals, let him be anathema" (Council of the Vatican I, *De Deo*. can. 3 & 4). Here again we see the restrictions of the spirit of alternatives, that is to say the inaptitude of reason for bringing together antinomian truths, whence the choice of the most important aspect — or the most opportune — to the detriment of secondary or inopportune truths. In reality, the fact that the world is in no way the divine Substance as such by no means prevents the cosmic substance from being in its own way a modality of the metacosmic Substance, without the reverse holding good: the Substance of God is in no way affected, either in the sense of extension or reduction, by the substance of the world; which substance is "in a certain way" something of the divine Substance, but the latter is in no way the former. The pot is of clay, clay is not the pot; only the doctrine of the degrees of Reality can account for this play of metaphysical relationships. But the chief consideration for theology is to prevent reason, to which it is generally addressed, from following its natural limitations in the face of mysteries and attributing to the world a directly Divine quality; reason, by its nature, has no simultaneous vision of realities which go beyond its range, so that antinomian expressions easily lead it into error. Reason obtains knowledge like a man walking about and exploring a countryside by successive discoveries, whereas the intellect contemplates the same countryside from a mountain height — an image inadequate in several respects, but nonetheless instructive as regards the essential point. Reason is capable of combining divergent perspectives within its own field, the natural or the general, but incapable of so doing beyond this level; now theology cannot presuppose direct intellection; it is always determined by three factors: dogma, from which it is derived, reason, to which it is a priori addressed, and the collectivity, whose spiritual interest is its own.

*

* *

Now, if a given form of evidence — not evidence in itself — cannot be polyvalent, human receptacles being providentially diverse, the same can be said of the persuasive value of an argument drawn from the historical and miraculous objects of faith; we mean that the superhuman and perfect character of the Man-God does not furnish an absolute argument against the sacred doctrines belonging to another perspective, any more than does the evidence of the Islamic testimony of Unity.[21] Indeed, a distinction must be made, in the case of the Man-God, between superhuman nature and terrestrial form or function; the function of Christ having been the Redemption, and therefore sacrifice, it was impossible for Him not to suffer, although, from the Buddhist point of view, for example, in which suffering

21. Jews and Christians will say that they possess the same evidence, but what is at issue here is the function that this evidence assumes in their spiritual perspectives. Judaism emphasizes the covenant between the unique God and His chosen people, while Christianity veils Unity in the Trinity; but in neither case is the metaphysical comprehension of Unity in question.

essentially is the ransom for the imperfection of existence, this capacity to suffer appears as an imperfection. This in no way means that Buddhism excludes an understanding of the express function which suffering, and therefore passibility, assumed for Christ, but solely that the Buddhist perspective starts from a truth for which the human position of Christ does not a priori present itself as being an intelligible aspect of perfection.[22] The converse is equally true, and that by the force of things: for the Christian perspective, the position of the Buddha has an aspect of imperfection, because of the apparently "rational" and "empirical" character of the Buddhist path, and despite the impassive serenity of the Blessed One, which here will seem like philosophical stoicism. Analogous comments could be applied to each of the great Messengers, notably also to the Prophet: from the Christian point of view he seems too earthly, whereas this aspect, to the extent that it corresponds to a reality and so loses any pejorative sense, results from the particular character of the mission of Muhammad, which consists in reintegrating the human into the universal rather than exclusively in introducing the divine into the human. If Islam does not misinterpret Christ as Christians misinterpret the Prophet, this is because the Person of Jesus has a place in Moslem dogma; however, while Christ is venerated in Islam as "Spirit of God" *(Rūh Allāh)* and "Seal of Sanctity," *(Khātam al-wilāyah)* He does

22. Meister Eckhart somewhere remarks that the movements of the soul in Christ and the Virgin were in no way contrary to impassibility, this not being a state of inertia. As an example, holy anger is a movement of concentration and not a going outside oneself; it is like an "incarnation" of the divine Wrath in the human microcosm, which must at that moment be free from passionate anger. The inner criterion of holy anger is precisely calmness, whereas passionate anger carries away the entire being and brings forgetfulness of God; it has no center, that is to say it is entirely peripheral and dissipated. Holy anger exists only by virtue of a motionless center, an implacable truth which determines it; when driving the money-changers from the Temple, Christ was impassible.

not appear in this perspective as "God," and from the Christian point of view this amounts to a complete denial. But it is not our purpose to enlarge on these divergencies; the essential point is to take note of a certain aspect of "non-perfection" — and there is no common measure between this aspect and human imperfections — which appears, from metaphysical necessity, in the outward function of the *Avatāra*. This truth can be illustrated as follows: if we start from the idea that the circle is the perfect geometrical figure, but that at the same time there must be different forms of perfection, we must conclude that no one of them can be another — otherwise they would not be different — and that, consequently, none of them can be the circle; however, each of the simple geometrical figures is perfect, without restriction, in relation to complex and asymmetrical figures, which here represent ordinary men. Let us say then that each *Avatāra* is intrinsically the circle, but that he is manifested by the force of things as a less perfect form; this form will nonetheless express circular perfection in the sense that each fundamental geometrical form — cross, square, triangle, spiral, pentagram — can be inscribed in a circle and manifests the circle's truth in its own way.

A distinction has been made above between the persuasive force of miracles as compared with intellectual evidence. These two positions, let us repeat, far from being mutually exclusive, always to some degree go hand in hand; it could be said, for example, that the objective or outward fact of Revelation is to the collectivity what the subjective or inward vision of intellection — in cases where it occurs — is to the individual. Thus both positions are true, each in its own way and within the framework of its ontological premises; and they are necessarily related, since on the one hand the sufficient reason of a miracle is to unveil an evidence, and on the other hand the miracle appears to intellectual certainty like a projection of itself onto the plane of facts and symbols.

*

* *

It is important to understand that dogmas possess, besides their doctrinal significance, a mystical or "alchemical" function, so that dogmatic divergencies — insofar as it is a question of intrinsic orthodoxy — correspond in a very broad sense to differences of spiritual method;[23] dogmas confer not only ideas, but also — and essentially — "ways of being." Certainly our confrontation of different dogmatic systems — which are so constructed as to exclude one another and to be ignorant of one another insofar as they are formal crystallizations — has something humanly "abnormal" about it, although doubtless it is inevitable in our times of universal intermingling and of cataloging all values. Indeed, man is made to know one sun alone and to live by it, and not to experience each of the innumerable suns of the galaxy and of other nebulae; Providence has enclosed man in one traditional system just as she has enclosed him in one solar system. But that does not alter the fact either that the diversity of spiritual systems is metaphysically as necessary as that of the cosmic systems, or that there are situations in which man cannot but be aware of this.

23. It is important not to confuse religious antagonisms with the clashes between the old civilizations and modern ideas which are so wrongly charged against Christianity. How can one not see, in the following passage from the Gospels, a prophetic allusion to a religious proselytism which, imbued as it is with the illusions of our times, spoils with one hand what it gives with the other: "Woe unto you, scribes and Pharisees, hypocrites! for ye compass sea and land to make one proselyte, and when he is made, ye make him twofold more the child of hell than yourselves" (Matt. 23:15).

Manifestations
of the Divine Principle

There is assuredly no common measure between the supreme Principle and its cosmic manifestation, for the latter is nothing of itself, whereas the Principle is only of itself and remains unaffected by its expressions; but since on our level of reality we do exist, there have to be possible points of contact between us and God; therefore the incommensurability between the two terms must in a certain way veil itself and does so precisely by way of those "points of intersection" which we can call "divine manifestations."

The Principle manifests itself not only as world, but also within the world, otherwise we would have no "reference point" in relation to the Infinite. To affirm that there is a cosmos is to say that the latter necessarily includes within itself manifestations of that which it manifests by its existence; the relationship God-world, Creator-creation, Principle-manifestation, is reflected in the creation itself, by reason of the homogeneity of reality and on pain of projecting us into an isolation — or a nothingness — that is ontologically inconceivable. But this does not mean that there could be, even on the plane of reflections, a kind of definitive symmetry between the Infinite and the finite; consequently, the manifestation of the Principle cannot be located at an absolutely defined point, and that is why it is necessary to distinguish, in what seems at first sight a purely verbal way, between the "manifestation of the Principle" and the "Principle manifested," according to whether the emphasis falls on "manifestation" or on "Principle." This distinction indicates that there is in the world no one unique and absolute "point of intersection" between the Divine and the human, that there is thus always a predominance of one or the other of the two "poles."[1] The same holds true, moreover, for all symbolism: a symbol can be interpreted either "horizontally" from the standpoint of analogy, or "vertically" from the standpoint of identity: it is the difference between concentric circles which reflect the center and radii which attain it.[2] In every case of a contact between the Divine and the terrestrial we see this fluctuation between the metaphysical perspective of essential — not "material" — identity and the cosmological perspective of analogy or of symbolical parallelism, hence of difference. This contact between the Divine and the human is, by reason of its very elusiveness, a mystery, and even the mystery par excellence, for we touch God "everywhere and nowhere," as Pascal would say. God is quite close to us, infinitely close, but we are far from Him; He is incarnate in a given symbol, but we risk grasping only the husk, retaining only the shadow. Idolatry, which divinizes the shadow as such, and atheism, which denies God by reason of His intangibility — but it is we who are "absent," not God — reduce to absurdity the two aspects of symbolism: identity, which is unitive, and analogy, which is separative, but parallel.

1. This is what explains on the one hand the "human" character of the Moslem conception of the Prophets — Muhammad and the other "Messengers" are "manifestation" not "Principle" — and on the other hand the divinity of Christ; He is "Principle" whether manifested or not. Let us note that the anti-incarnationist perspective of Islam does not exclude the fact of the *Avatāra*, but gives it at most an accentuation which veils it in the name of the oneness and transcendence of God.

2. This does not imply that the principle of analogy does not operate between different horizontal levels.

In order to clarify metaphysically the problem of divine manifestation as such, one must start by considering that which, in the Principle itself, prefigures it, namely Being, which is distinguished by its auto-determination from Non-Being (or Beyond-Being). It could thus be said, in a certain sense, that Being is the "manifestation" — but in divinis — of Beyond-Being, which alone is "absolutely infinite," if such a paradoxical expression be permissible; Being — the "personal God" — will be infinite in relation to cosmic manifestation, but not in relation to Beyond-Being, which is the divine suprapersonal Essence; in itself, Being can be defined as "neither finite, nor infinite," or as "non-finite, non-infinite," verbal nuances which are far from useless for him who fathoms their meaning.

Being, so to speak, polarizes into Creative Act and *Materia prima* (the couple Purusha-Prakriti of Hindu doctrine); it conceives and produces the Creation, which is none other than Its own projection outside Itself, or Its manifestation. But words are not adequate to give an account, on their own plane, of the divine Principle; they can do no more than act as quite provisional supports for a "recalling," in the intellect, of what is inherent in it from all eternity according to its very nature. When we speak of "projection outside Itself," it is understood that nothing is outside God, and that nothing can affect the divine immutability; but the complexity of the Real allows — and obliges — us to use images that are doubtless in themselves contradictory and "non-logical," but in no way illogical.

The ontological bipolarization just mentioned is reflected not only in the distinction "Principle-manifestation," but also within manifestation itself, in the distinction between the Universal Spirit and total Creation, the Spirit being the center of the Creation.

*

* *

Among the innumerable divine manifestations which pierce the veil of Existence in an endless variety of modes — some direct, others indirect — there are those which can be considered as fundamental, namely Creation, the Universal Spirit, Man, the Intellect, the *Avatāra*, Revelation, the Symbol and Grace.

Creation is the great "objectification" of the Divine Subject; it is the divine manifestation par excellence. It has a beginning and an end insofar as a particular cycle is envisaged, but it is in itself a permanent divine possibility, a metaphysically necessary objectification of the divine infinity; to deny the necessity of the creation would amount to attributing arbitrariness to the Divinity. God is free in his infinity which pierces through everywhere, but liberty could not interfere with necessity, a perfection which derives from the quality of absoluteness; in a word, one must not confuse either divine Liberty with human arbitrariness, or divine Necessity with human constraint; God is both absolute and infinite. Creation is perfect by its very oneness and totality, it reabsorbs in its perfection all partial disequilibria; thus it is that Existence is "Virgin" and "Mother," and that it is merciful. The Virgin Mary incarnates Existence[3] and objectifies all its perfections: beauty, purity, mercy.

The Universal Spirit is the divine Intelligence incarnate in Existence; it is like the reflection of the divine Sun in the cosmic Substance: God projects Himself, so to speak, into that "void" or "nothingness" which is the plane of the creature.[4] He creates Himself, it might be said, as "the Spirit of God" moving "upon the face of the waters," and

3. By "Existence" we always mean the cosmic Substance which is at the same time creative and virginal, and not a principle which would embrace God, for the latter is "Being" and "Beyond-Being." God is not "existent" but "non-inexistent," that is to say "supra-ontological" and a fortiori "supra-existential."

4. That is to say, He "first produces the Waters in which He lays a seed; this then becomes an egg shining like gold, as dazzling as the star of a

it is from these — from the chaos of cosmic possibilities — that He causes the world to come forth. This Spirit is thus the divine Intellect immanent in the Cosmos, of which It constitutes the center and the heart; It penetrates as by innumerable arteries of light into all realms — or into all microcosms — of the manifested Universe; it is thus that God is present at the center of everything. This projection — or this "unveiling" *(tajallī)* as the Sufis would say — is "intellectual" in the sense that it proceeds from the aspect "Intellect" of God *(Chit* in Sanskrit), whereas the total Creation — of which the Spirit is the center — is "existential" because it proceeds from the aspect "Being" *(Sat)*. In the Spirit, God manifests Himself as Center and Light; in the Creation, He manifests Himself as Totality and Life.

These two divine manifestations, Creation and the Universal Spirit, are of the macrocosmic order: the first constitutes the macrocosm itself, and the second is its intellective and divine center. We will now consider the analogous manifestations in the realm of microcosms.

*
*   *

Man is a divine manifestation, not in his accidentality and his fallen state, but in his theomorphism and his primordial and principial perfection. He is the "field of manifestation" of the intellect, which reflects the universal Spirit and thereby the divine Intellect; man as such reflects the cosmic totality, the Creation, and thereby the Being of God. The divine Intelligence confers on man intellect, reason and free will; it is by these features — and by speech which manifests them — that the human being is distinguished from animals in a "relatively absolute" fashion; it

thousand rays, and in this the supreme Being gives birth to Himself in the form of Brahma, the forefather of all beings" *(Mānava-Dharma-Shāstra,* I, 8 and 9).

is true that every intelligence, even that of plants, is "intellect," but the human intellect alone is direct and transcendent; it alone has access to the Divine. The quasi-divine character of man — which still asserts itself in sacred and primordial collectivities — implies that it is impossible to "realize God" without first realizing the human norm; consequently, this norm is "Prophet" in relation to the fallen individual.

The question of free will just alluded to leads us to point out that if man were in no way free, as some maintain, there would be no difference between a man acting under constraint and a man acting freely, or between a chained animal and another free to move; the word "liberty" would not even exist. Conversely, if man were in no way determined, as some also hold — for there is no possible error which does not show itself somewhere — he would be able to change his form, his race or the day of his birth; this means that the truth lies between the two extremes, or between two absurdities.

Man being "made of clay" is corruptible, whence the necessity of his redemption.[5] Non-formal manifestation is beyond corruptibility, or rather it is corruptible only at a single point, or "just once" — at the fall of Lucifer — for the corruptibility inherent in the formal world presupposes a corrupted essence which makes corruptibility possible, an essence which in relation to man is personified by Satan. Lucifer being an essence — that is to say something which is "totally itself" — cannot be converted,[6] but man, who is

5. For non-Christian exoterism, generally speaking, human theomorphism already comprises of itself what Christians call the "redemption," namely the possibility of a "return to God;" being a man is in itself enough to offer a chance of salvation. The initiatic framework of Christianity excludes this manner of seeing things; for the Christian, man is truly born through baptism alone.

6. Satan not being a person, Origen speaks of the "destruction" of "Death" and not of the conversion of the devil; nonetheless, this final destruction is not total annihilation, for what is destroyed is not the actual

a form, and thus something which is "not altogether itself" — the "itself" here being divine — can be converted "to himself" or to his divine nature, in the likeness of Adam, just as he can become identified with the satanic essence if he detaches his form from its divine Essence.[7] Damnation is the fall of the form which denies its essence; with the devil the case is the reverse, for he is an essence who denied the "form of God" in refusing to worship Adam.[8] The ambiguity of the human state is that we are as it were suspended between God — our Essence — and the human form, which is "made of clay"; we are so to speak a mixture of divinity and dust. To say that Man is a form is to say that to some extent he falls under the domination of the "demiurgic" essence which hardens and separates, and which is the

substance of the powers of evil, but their state of perversion. Apocatastasis is a transmutation which implies no "personal" reintegration. Among the angels — good or bad — personifications are in fact only "accidental," and related to their contacts with the human world.

7. The essence of Angels — except in the case of the supreme or "central" Angels — is not directly God, but the divine Attributes; the Angels are, however, superior to men by their character of being pure essences, or in other words, by the absence of formal crystalliaztion: man is their superior by his central position, and that is why Brahmins can "command" the *devas*. As for the supreme Angels, we have spoken of them in the chapter *"An-Nūr"* in our book, *Dimensions of Islam*.

8. This is the doctrine of the fall of Iblis. It is to be noted that according to the Koran Iblis was "created of fire" and that he is therefore a *jinn*, that is, not a "luminous" but an "igneous" being. In Hindu terms, we would say that *tamas* (the principle of darkness, of "earth," of existential "hardening," of ignorance) derives indirectly, by "detaching" itself, from *rajas* (the principle of "fire," of existential "expansion," of passion), which in its turn proceeds, in an equally "oblique" manner, from *sattva* (the principle of luminosity, of spiritual "transparency," of knowledge). The name Lucifer indicates that the spirit of evil proceeds — evidently by falling, and thus indirectly — from the "support of light," that is to say from *sattva;* in this perspective, the intermediary *rajas* is assimilated to *tamas*, exactly as, from the point of view of knowledge, passion is assimilable to ignorance, although the difference between these two terms remains real on their own level.

principle of individuation insofar as it is dark and subversive. Satan is the passional aspect of this principle, and in fact those men are lost who put their passion into egocentric hardness — whence by compensation their intellectual softness — and who find their satisfaction in rage against the universal "Otherness," the necessarily objective Truth, and so against everything opposed to their own subjectivity which is itself both hardened and passional;[9] that is why Dante's hell contains both fire and ice. In the hereafter, where the reality of human positions is laid bare, this rage is like a joy which tears apart, the joy being in the subjective passion, and the tearing in the objective reality; hell is as it were the revolt of nothingness, it is the nothingness which seeks to be the All.[10] When man turns away from his divine Essence, his ego becomes like a stone pulling him downwards, and his Essence turns away from him; what then fills this vacuum is the dark essence, that of formal compression and of the fall.

But what we would like to consider now is the actual appearance of man, his physical quality of "image of God," which distinguishes him a priori from all other creatures on earth, so that to speak of the human body is almost to speak of man as such. Our bodily form would in fact be unintelligible if it were not for our faculties of intelligence and liberty; it is on the contrary explicable only through these qualities. Let us say at once that the profanation of human

9. This passional tendency to condensation, separation and fall can be founded on very diverse attitudes; it can be located in thought or in the flesh; idolatry of the latter can be as mortal, or nearly so, as rejection of the Truth, not to mention malice, in which the combination of hardening and passion is particularly obvious.

10. Boehme, and in Islam Al-Jili, have very rightly insisted on this aspect of enjoyment attaching to infernal states. Let us remark here that if hell were eternal in the true sense of the word, instead of being simply perpetual and so perishing with duration, the devil would be partly right in his pretension to divinity; but this is impossible, since "nothingness" cannot "be".

beauty by the passions in no way authorizes contempt for this work of the Creator: despite the good intentions of those who seek to defend virtue at the expense of truth and intelligence, to calumniate this beauty is a kind of blasphemy and all the more so since the *Avatāra* of necessarily synthesises the total Creation in his body and — what is tantamount to the same thing — in its beauty. Some will doubtless insist that all earthly beauty is imperfect or carries blemishes, but this is false insofar as they go on to deduce from this that there is no true beauty on earth. On the other hand, if earthly beauty can be perfect in its kind, it is nonetheless exclusive of other kinds, and so in a certain sense limited: the beauty of a rose cannot realize that of a water-lily, and in the same way human beauties, whether individual or racial, exclude one another; God alone possesses simultaneously all possible beauty, the Essence being beyond the segmentation of form.

What constitutes the theomorphism of the human body is its quality of totality and its nobility: its totality is shown above all in the richness — or the universality — of its faculties insofar as this determines bodily structure; and its nobility, by its vertical — and so celestial — position and its gait which is free and sovereign because detached from the ground. Certain animal species do indeed have nobility — the same can be said of certain vegetable and mineral species — but they are fragmentary in comparison to man and therefore lack totality. The case of monkeys is the opposite, in the sense that they certainly possess physical totality, or nearly so, but they lack nobility, that is to say they are not fashioned either for the human gait, nor for the human carriage of the head, defects which suffice to rivet them to animality. The monkey is man prefigured as regards animality alone, while in the human brute the animality devours the man; in such a brute, humanity is like an accident.

In man alone is the head "freed" from the body and dominates it, as if it were a new and autonomous being, like the Spirit dominating chaos.[11] In the opposition between the head and the body — and each appears as a world unto itself — the head represents man, Consciousness, and the body woman, Existence; but the whole body assumes a feminine aspect when it is opposed to the heart, which then denotes the divine Intellect, in relation to which the creature — mental as well as corporal — appears in its dependent and lunar nature.[12]

The question of human theomorphism raises that of the bodily and mental difference between the sexes, since each of these is theomorphic while being distinct from the opposite sex. The male body appears like a revelation of the Spirit, it evinces intelligence, victorious strength, impassibility, active perfection; the female body is like a revelation of Existence, it reveals Substance — or Totality, not Centrality, as does the male body — and it evinces beauty, moving innocence, fecundity, passive perfection.

11. Nevertheless, infra-human creatures should not be underestimated. The classical example of a "homocentrism" that is metaphysically inadmissible, though doubtless opportune in certain perspectives, is the opinion according to which animals and plants were created with the sole object of preserving man's animal life, as though all plants and all animals were useful to man, and as though this usefulness explained the forms, colors and other infinitely varied features of these beings, not to speak of the psychological individuality and the contemplative side of the higher animals. Moreover all these aspects are largely useless to the subsistence of the animals and plants themselves. The fact that the lion firstly is not useful to man, and secondly possesses a mane which is not useful for his own subsistence shows in its way that the animal has an end independent of his material life on the one hand and of utility to man on the other; no doubt he does not possess reason, but he has consciousness, which also transcends crude matter; now a consciousness cannot have its end in the unconscious; everything in nature is made "to praise God."

12. On this subject, see F. Schuon, *Gnosis: Divine Wisdom*, the chapter "Ternary Aspect of the Human Microcosm" (Perennial Books, 1990).

Man expresses — always within the same framework of human theomorphism which confers on both sexes the same character of center and of totality, setting aside any question of predominance — man, then, expresses knowledge and woman love. Also, the masculine body is more "geometrical" — it is in a way the "abstract" image of the divine Person — while the feminine body is "musical" and appears as a "concrete" expression of our existential Substance and, *in divinis,* of the infinite Beatitude. The feminine body is compounded of nobility and innocence, that is, it is noble by its theomorphism — in this respect it is not distinct from the masculine body, except in its mode — and innocent because it reflects the innocence of existence; its nobility it manifests by its vertical lines, and its innocent fecundity by its curves, and thus it bears in its flesh the fundamental aspects of the *Materia Prima:* the loftiness, purity and mercy of the *Virgo Genitrix,* "full of grace." The beauty of woman appears to man as the revelation of the blissful Essence of which he is himself as it were a crystallization — in this respect femininity transcends man — and this explains the alchemical role and the "solvent" power of woman's beauty: the vibratory shock of the "aesthetic event" — in the deepest sense of this expression — should be the means of "liquefaction of the hardened heart," whereas passional emotion, when its "idolatrous" side is not neutralized by a traditional consecration, cannot be exempt from a chaotic and, in principle, promethean and mortal animality. And here it may be pointed out that, from a spiritual point of view, the body has something of a two-edged sword: it may be the vehicle of a consciousness of being, a contemplative non-thought or a kind of ontological and blessed calm, but also of a merely physical and sensual assurance; the body is then lived with a view to existence and not to pure Being. The opportuneness of a contemplative junction between the bodily and the spiritual — and we are not here thinking primarily of sexuality —

will thus depend on individual as well as collective mental structures.[13]

The human being is compounded of geometry and music, of spirit and soul, of virility and femininity: by geometry, he brings the chaos of existence back to order, that is he brings blind substance back to its ontological meaning and thus constitutes a reference point between Earth and Heaven, a "sign-post" pointing towards God; by music he brings the segmentation of form back to unitive life, reducing form, which is a death, to Essence — at least symbolically and virtually — so that it vibrates with a joy which is at the same time a nostalgia for the Infinite.[14] As symbols, the masculine body indicates a victory of the Spirit over chaos, and the feminine body, a deliverance of form by Essence; the first is like a magic sign which would subjugate the blind forces of the Universe, and the second like celestial music which would give back to fallen matter its paradisiac transparency, or which, to use the language of Taoism, would make trees flower beneath the snow.

Matter can indeed assume a divine form but this form must be "blighted" by afflictions recalling its exile. The human body has something of the divine by reason of its theomorphism, so that it risks feeling itself God — or being

13. Hatha-yoga is a kind of "corporal-existential thought" which would be not only impracticable, but even inconceivable in a people afflicted with vestimentary moralism.

14. This function of reducing formal crystallizations to the Essence shows well the symbolic correspondence between woman and wine, or between love and drunkenness. Dissolution downwards, towards infraformal, dark and chaotic essences, gives rise to many illusions, which explains why exoterism cannot make use of certain symbols. Geometrical coordination moreover can also give rise to sinister counterfeits, namely to limitative crystallizations of the mind, to a spirit of systematization and partition, to the "logical error" which denies and compromises the non-formal clarities of the Essence; it is these latter that are then falsely identified with chaos, while form becomes a synonym of the Absolute; the idea of the Infinite is replaced by that of Perfection or of Being, as is shown by certain aspects of "classical" thought.

deified — if it is not humbled in its very existence. We meet everywhere in nature this humiliation of the theomorphic, for example in the fact that the sun, the physical reflection of the divine Intellect, has to set "in order to prostrate itself," as Moslems put it, "before the throne of *Allāh.*" In all cases of this kind — direct theomorphism on the one hand and existential humiliation on the other — spiritual significance coincides with physical necessity; the latter could never furnish a sufficient explanation of the imperfections in question, precisely because it presupposes metaphysical conditions without which it would itself have no existence. We will add that the devil has every interest in making us believe that physical animality is what we are,[15] that there is here a kind of squalid accident in creation, as if natural blemishes did not, on the contrary, remind us that we are other than this and that our homeland is elsewhere. There is no reason for asking whether it is nature which by its impurities mocks man, or whether it is man who by his prejudices mocks nature; man is not "of this world," and it is the world which, in the Name of God makes him aware of this, for nothing is chance, all is a divine message. Nothing so purifies us from the psychic traces of our materiality as consciousness of the profound necessity of things, as also of their nothingness.

*

* *

At man's center there dwells another divine manifestation: the Intellect. Intellect is that in man which participates in the divine Subject, and which therefore can be called "uncreate and uncreatable," to use an expression of Meister Eckhart: it is like the permanent manifestation of the divine in the human microcosm — permanent, but

15. This is the opposite of the Vedantic: "I am neither this body, nor this ego. . . ." The Vedanta expressly mentions the conviction, "I am the body," as being the doctrine of the demons.

most often obscured and rendered inoperative. The Intellect is in subjective mode what Revelation is in objective mode; but the latter is transmissible, whereas Knowledge in itself is incommunicable. The "uncreate" character which certain theologians, Christian and Moslem alike, discern in faith indicates that the latter is an aspect of the Intellect: it is an indirect intellection, passive and formal no doubt, but an adherence to the uncreate Truth nonetheless, and so a participation or, to use a rather paradoxical expression, a "mode of identity."

As this question of the Intellect has been sufficiently dealt with at the beginning of this book, and also in the course of all our previous works, it will not be pursued here and another manifestation of the divine Principle will now be considered: this is Revelation or — what in some cases comes to the same thing — Incarnation, the *Avatāra*. If the Universal Spirit is the reflection of the divine in Creation, and Intellect the reflection of the divine in man — Creation and man being themselves divine reflections, the first in "nothingness" and the second among terrestrial beings — Revelation, in turn, will be the reflection of the divine in humanity. But while the Intellect is subjective by its participation in the divine Subject and man is objective as being a form of existence, the *Avatāra* is subjective in relation to Creation in that he personifies it in a human subject, and Revelation is objective in relation to the Intellect in that it crystallizes the latter through the medium of a form, a symbolism, a system of expressions. In other words, the Intellect "objectifies itself" by Revelation, and Creation "subjectifies itself" by Incarnation. By the fall, the Intellect, which in itself is universal, individualized itself and gave rise to reason, whereas Creation, which a priori was conceived by man as "inward," exteriorized itself and became the material world. The *Avatāra*, in subjectifying the Universe and in objectifying the Intellect, restores to man in a certain way his primordial quality of effective and conscious manifestation of the divine; Creation is what is most "outward"; the two poles meet fully in the *Avatāra,* who thus unites in his person both the totality of the objective macrocosm, and the center of the subjective microcosm.

It is obvious that one divine manifestation cannot be defined simply as the reflection of another divine manifestation; each, whether it be macrocosmic or microcosmic, manifests God in its own right. The *Avatāra* "incarnates" God, while also personifying — since he is in the world — Creation, Universal Spirit, Man and Intellect; if he incarnates God he cannot be other than perfect, and if he is perfect — and he is so by definition — he cannot but incarnate the total cosmos, the primary manifestation of the Principle, with the subsequent manifestations that it implies. That God should incarnate Himself in man[16] proves moreover that the human species is itself, in a given world — this one of ours — a divine manifestation with respect to the peripheral beings which surround it, as explained above; but the fact of this incarnation proves also that the divinity of man has become inoperative, that it resides now only in the impersonal design of humanity, not in the individual as such, nor, of course, in the quantitative collectivity, otherwise the Incarnation would constitute a kind of pleonasm. Moreover, man is not an absolute pole of the cosmos; he is the center of the terrestrial world as the sun is the center of our planetary system, without thereby excluding the existence of other suns and other systems; and the fact that man as such represents only "one world" and not "the World," shows again that there is no symmetry between the Infinite and the finite, and that the center of the latter is "everywhere and nowhere," to use once again Pascal's expression. Man is

16. As regards the earlier *Avatāras* of Vishnu, their animal symbolism must not be taken literally.

one of the microcosms which reflect at the same time — in a direct and integral manner[17] — the Center and the Totality, the Spirit and the Universe; in other worlds, this central — and relatively "unique" — function must fall to other beings, analogous to man only in their central and total character, beings we shall doubtless never know. And this is important: the fact that man is center and totality, so that God can be incarnate in him, proves that he is in no way subject to any essential and transforming evolution, changing the very constants of his form to the point of separating him from present-day man as much as the latter is separated from the ape; this is quite impossible, for the Infinite incarnates in the finite only in function of an absolute character, which can indeed disappear, but cannot change in its essence and its archetype.

The *Avatāra* coincides with Revelation, with Tradition; Revelation means that God has said "I," that He has revealed Himself to some human receptacle, to some section of humanity. Every religion therefore presents itself as something absolute, and this is strictly comparable with our empirical subjectivity, the unique, exclusive and irreplaceable — though logically contradictory — character of the ego. The ego is in practice "solipsist," just as, in theory, religion is; it is forced to admit the existence of other egos,[18] but it cannot abolish the actual subjectivity and the empirical uniqueness of its own "I," even though the plurality of egos is as unintelligible, humanly and concretely, as the limitlessness of time and space: it is in vain that man establishes, thanks to the objectivity of his intelligence, that the "other" is also an "I"; he cannot grasp with either his

17. This has to be pointed out because the sun, for example, or gold, or a given body in some realm or another equally represents the Center or Totality, but in a manner that is indirect, partial and quite passive.

18. It is this moreover which distinguishes the human ego from the animal ego; to say man is to say objectivity, at any rate in relation to what we are concerned with here.

reason or his imagination why it is "I" who am "I," and why "the other" is "the other." Whatever man may do there is in egoity something insoluble, irreducible, not to say absurd, from the human point of view of course; this shows that a streak of absurdity, or let us say illusion, enters inevitably into the structure of the cosmos. All relative subjectivity is contradictory, since it is "objectivity" in relation to the pure Subject; the latter — the divine Self — "contains" all particular subjects while infinitely transcending them. It alone is without contradiction and therefore without illusion.

But let us return to the de facto "egoity" of Revelations: it is explained not only by the divine unity and the absoluteness of the Word, but also — insofar as it involves a restriction — by the human milieu, which is formal, thus exclusive, and at the same time differentiated, thus also diverse and multiple. Moreover it must be understood that for God only essential and spiritually efficacious truth is fully true; that is to say, crude fact is nothing outside that truth. There are here dimensions of truth superimposed on one another, and this resolves the problem of the apparent contradictions met with in the Scriptures, or in one and the same dogmatic system, for example the inevitable question of freedom and predestination.[19] Facts count here only in respect of their symbolism and possibly their causal or sacramental role.

*

* *

It will perhaps be useful to make clear that, as regards the *Avatāra,* one may distinguish broadly speaking four categories of incarnation, two of them "major" and two "minor,"

19. Or the abolition — in practice if not in theory — of the Torah, however "eternal," by Christianity, even though Christ did "not come to destroy, but to fulfil"; the antithesis nonetheless subsists on the non-esoteric level.

each of the two groups comprising a "plenary" and a "partial" incarnation. The major *Avatāras* are the founders of religions or, in circumstances where the question of a renewal of form could not arise, the supreme dispensers of grace, such as Rama and Krishna; among these founders or dispensers, some are "solar" and others "lunar" manifestations of the Divinity, depending on the form of the Message, and so also on the nature of the collectivity receiving it. The minor *Avatāras* are also sub-divided into plenary or solar and partial or lunar: these are the great sages or saints who, within the framework of a given tradition and consequently on a lesser scale, repeat the function of the major *Avatāras* in a manner either solar[20] or lunar; there are also feminine incarnations, but their role — that of *shakti* — is always relatively secondary, whatever the level of their manifestation. If Hinduism attributes the major incarnations to Vishnu and the minor incarnations rather to Shiva, this is doubtless because the major Messages — the religions — being addressed to whole collectivities and creating civilizations, perform the work of "conservation," whereas the minor Messages — particular doctrines or methods — have a "transforming" function.[21] Finally, if the major *Avatāras* are symbolically ten in number — the number of the total cycle — while the minor *Avatāras* are in principle innumerable, this is because the supreme Messages coincide with cyclic epochs and may govern some thousands of years,

20. "On this side (the western flank of Subiaco) where it loses its violence (where the slope becomes gentle) a sun (Saint Francis) was born to the world, like that which sometimes rises out of the Ganges (where its rising is most brilliant). May he then who wishes to speak of this place, not call it Assisi, which would be too little; let him call it the East, if he wants the proper word." (Dante, *Paradiso*, XI: *Di questa costa, là dov'ella frange — Più sua rattezza, nacque al mondo un sole — Come fa questo talvolta di Gange — Però chi d'esso loco fa parole — Non dica Ascesi, chè direbbe corto — Ma Oriente, se proprio dir vuole.*)

21. According to an opinion widely accepted in India, Shri Shankara is a particularly eminent "descent" of Shiva.

which is not the case for the work of sages and saints, whose task is to actualize an ever-present Spirit.[22]

*

* *

These considerations relating to the *Avatāra* lead us to deal briefly with the creation of man — and indeed with Creation as such — and with the evolutionary theories attached to it in the minds of the majority today.

According to a Red Indian myth, the Great Spirit created man three times over, each time destroying what He had made before; the first two attempts were abortive; only the third was to survive.[23] The various forms of animal fossils (gigantic saurians and so forth) prove, not a generic continuity between species, but first efforts towards incarnating certain "ideas" out of the primordial chaos. During the epoch of the great waves of Creation, "matter" was not yet definitely separated from the subtle world, to which, for example, the psychic elements belong, whether they be

22. According to some texts, the "descents" of Vishnu are much more numerous — not to mention the various incarnations of other divinities, such as Indra, Agni, Varuna, Yama — but we must limit ourselves here to the essential aspects of the problem, at the risk of seeming systematic. In relation to the "avataric" character of Plato and Alexander — Pythagoras could even more properly be included as well as certain heroes in mythology — we would underline the following: there is a providential relationship — as regards area of expansion and preparation of environment — between Caesar and Christianity on the one hand and between Alexander and Islam on the other; Caesar is mentioned in the Gospels and Alexander in the Koran. This shows that the mission of the minor and lunar *Avatāra* can lie on the political plane — but on a very vast scale — without implying a properly spiritual Message.

23. This myth coincides in a remarkable way with the teaching of the *Saura-Purāna:* while Shiva, as Kala, was meditating on the new Creation — after the destruction of the old one, or rather its reabsorption into Prakriti — there appeared first of all the elements deriving from tamas, namely darkness, blindness, ignorance, inertia. This Creation being insufficient, a new one was conceived, and so on until man.

conceived in subjective or objective mode;[24] Creation could thus take place, not by "evolution" starting from a single cell — an impossible hypothesis, anyway, and one which only pushes the limits of the difficulty further back — but by successive manifestations or materializations starting from the subtle state, the cosmic matrix of "ideas" to be incarnated.[25] This way of seeing things does not exclude very partial evolutions, or adaptations to environment, but reduces them to proportions compatible with metaphysical and cosmological principles.[26]

Ancient and medieval narratives furnish many illustrations — convincing for those who conceive this order of possibilities — of this "transparency" of matter, or of this interpenetration of material and subtle states: Angels and spirits manifested themselves readily in those days, given certain conditions; the marvelous was "the order of the day" it might be said; matter was not yet the impenetrable shell which it has become in the course of the last thousand years, and above all in the course of these last centuries, correlatively with the mental hardening of men. In primordial ages, cosmic analogies were still much more direct than later: the sun was much more directly "divine" than in more "solidified" ages and the same remark holds good for all the salient phenomena of nature: stars, elements, mountains, rivers, lakes, forests,

24. The world was not yet "solidified" as Guénon would say. See on this subject, as also on questions of "sacred geography," his *The Reign of Quantity* (Luzac, 1953) and our *Spiritual Perspectives and Human Facts* (Perennial Books, 1987).

25. Such things can still take place today, *mutatis mutandis,* under exceptional conditions and on a very restricted scale, in magical — or "spiritualistic" — operations, in which objects may "dematerialize" and "rematerialize," and psychic influences can assume human forms. The "ectoplasm" of seances is like a magical and shapeless imitation of primordial matter.

26. It is quite wrong to assume, as does a still widely current view, that it is only religious opinion which is opposed to evolutionism.

stones, plants, animals; "sacred geography" still kept all its
spiritual efficacy.

Creation — or "creations" — should then be represented not as a process of transformism taking place in
"matter" in the naively empirical sense of the word, but
rather as an elaboration by the life-principle, that is to say,
something rather like the more or less discontinuous pro-
ductions of the imagination: images arise in the soul from
a non-formal substance with no apparent link between
them; it is not the images which transform themselves, it is
the animic substance which causes their arising and creates
them. That man should appear to be the logical issue, not
indeed of an evolution, but of a series of "sketches" more
and more centered on the human form — sketches of
which the apes seem to represent disparate vestiges — this
fact, or this hypothesis, in no way signifies that there is any
common measure, thus a kind of psychological continuity,
between man and the anthropomorphic and in some sense
"embryonic" bodies which may have preceded him. The
coming of man is a sudden "descent" of the Spirit into a
receptacle that is perfect and definitive because it conforms
to the manifestation of the Absolute; the absoluteness of
man is like that of the geometrical point, which, strictly
speaking, is quantitatively unattainable starting from the
circumference.[27]

But let us return after this digression to the question of
divine manifestations. It remains to speak of the Symbol

27. The same thing is repeated in the womb: as soon as the body is
formed the immortal soul is suddenly fixed in it like a flash of lightning,
so that there is complete discontinuity between this new being and the
embryonic phases which have prepared its coming. It has quite rightly
been maintained, against transformism, not only that "the greater cannot
come from the less" (Guénon), but also that even though something
existent may gain more precision or become atrophied, there cannot on
the other hand be a motive, in a species, for the adjunction of a new
element, not to mention that nothing could guarantee the hereditary
character of such an element (according to Schubert-Soldern).

and of Grace: the latter is inward and non-formal, the former is outward and formal. Every form which expresses God — whether naturally or traditionally, but not artificially — is a symbol having power to save, in other words it can be a vehicle of, and a key to, Grace; in Grace, God is manifest not as form, but as presence or essence. Grace, Revelation, Intellect, and the Universal Spirit, can be called "uncreate," considering the essential identity which unites them to their divine Source; and by extension the same could be said of their respective receptacles, the symbol, the *Avatāra*, man, Creation — to specify their function — if this did not involve a contradiction in terms or if one could risk the expression "uncreate created." In fact, it is by this antinomic expression that the total Creation could legitimately be distinguished from any individual creature, or man from the animals, or the *Avatāra* from fallen humanity, or the symbol from arbitrary or artificial forms; but this would imply an ellipsis which would do too much violence to reason and language. Moreover a distinction must be made between two kinds of symbols: those of nature and those of Revelation; the first have spiritual efficacy only by virtue of their "consecration" or "revalorization" by the *Avatāra* or the revealed Word, or by virtue of a very exalted degree of knowledge which restores to them their fundamental reality. Before the Fall, every river was the Ganges, and every mountain was Kailasa, because the Creation was still "inward," the knowledge of good and evil not having yet "exteriorized" or "materialized" it, and likewise: for the sage, every river is a river of Paradise. Natural symbolism, which assimilates for example the sun to the divine Principle, derives from a "horizontal" correspondence; revealed symbolism, which makes this assimilation spiritually effective — in ancient solar cults and before their "petrifaction" — derives from a "vertical" correspondence; and likewise for gnosis, which reduces phenomena to ideas or archetypes. Much could be said here on the natural symbolism of bread and wine — or of body and blood — and their sacramentalization by Christ; likewise the sign of the Cross, which expresses with its two dimensions the respective mysteries of the Body-Bread and of the Blood-Wine, has of course always had its metaphysical meaning but received its quasi-sacramental virtue — at least in its specifically Christian form — through the incarnate Word; that is to say that it is necessary for the *Avatāra* to "live" a form in order to make it effective, and that therefore sacred formulae or divine Names must come from Revelation in order to be capable of being "realized."[28]

Just as there are two kinds of symbols there are two kinds of graces: natural graces, which are accessible to us on the basis of our very existence — through the virtues for example, or even in an apparently quite gratuitous manner, or through "sensible consolations" — and supernatural graces, which occur in direct or indirect connection with the various means of a Revelation, or which come from intellection; these graces are supernatural because they do not come from "cosmic reserves" but from the divine Source, "vertically" therefore and not "horizontally."[29]

It could be asked whether graces and symbols deriving from nature still deserve to be ranked as divine manifestations; they deserve it in principle and in a very broad sense, too broad doubtless to be safe from all accusations of abuse of language. It is obvious that every good, whether it be of an objective or subjective kind, can come only from God, but account must be taken of the fact that man is no longer capable of seeing spontaneously the celestial Cause in the

28. For example, rites of ablution whether Brahminical, Jewish, Christian or Islamic, draw their efficacy not from water as such — for this is "dead," "exteriorized" or "materialized" since the fall from the Edenic state — but from its consecration by the respective Revelation, which restores to water, within the framework of certain conditions, its primordial virtue.

29. In Moslem terms, this is the difference between the "blessing" (*ṣalāt*) and the "peace" (*salām*) which accompany the name of the Prophet.

terrestrial effect; thus God must be incarnated anew in forms that have become emptied or dead, at least in cases where this revalorization is imperative. This reservation signifies that the Intellect certainly possesses, in principle, the same powers as Revelation, but since Revelation exists, these powers cannot be actualized in opposition to it within the framework of a given Tradition; in fact, there is little likelihood of the intellect being actualized without the help of this framework, or of such frameworks if several traditional sources are available.[30]

30. Such is the case, for example, with those Christians who were Platonists or Neo-Platonists, and so nourished to one degree or another on Orphic and Pythagorean wisdom.

Complexity of the Concept
of Charity

Most of our contemporaries seem to forget that in true charity God is "served first," as Joan of Arc used to say: in other words they forget that charity is, in essence, to love God more than ourselves, to love our neighbor as ourselves, thus to love ourselves, but less than God; not to love our neighbor more than ourselves, and not to feel ourselves obliged to give him what, in our opinion, we would not deserve if we were in his place. Love of God possesses an element of the absolute deriving from the divine Absoluteness, but love for the neighbor — and love for ourselves — although recalling the relationship between man and God, has a relative character deriving from human relativity; the relationship remains similar thanks to the analogy, but the mode changes with the object.

To love God does not mean to cultivate a sentiment — that is to say, something which we enjoy without knowing whether God enjoys it — but rather to eliminate from the soul what prevents God from entering it; or again, it is to realize in ourselves that which, by virtue of the analogical correspondences, is conformable to the divine Presence. To love one's neighbor — and it is necessary to love him as an aspect of our love for God and by virtue of God's love for us — is to place oneself in the other, to abolish the illusory distinction between me and you, just as to love God is at bottom to abolish the separation which makes us remote from Him. Love for the neighbor indirectly effects the divine Presence in us: when man places himself in the neighbor, God places Himself in man; to abolish what separates us from the neighbor is to abolish what separates us from God.

*

* *

This can also be expressed as follows: if we must love God, and love Him more than ourselves and our neighbor, it is because love exists prior to ourselves and because we are issued from it; we love by virtue of our very existence. In the final analysis, we love only by God and for God; now it is quite evidently illogical to love ephemeral effects outside their immutable Cause; on the other hand, whoever loves the Cause thereby loves that which makes the effects lovable, namely the Cause which manifests itself in them through their qualities. To love creatures outside God is as senseless as wishing to enclose the sun's rays in a box.

Now, if in loving the divine Cause we love that which makes things on earth lovable, this love for the Cause demands from us love for the effects, not for their sakes nor for our own, but out of love for the Cause. Passion for the creature removes from love its real object and sufficient reason, it constitutes therefore no part of charity; he who loves the effect for itself, loves it precisely not as an effect, but as a cause, and that is to take the creature for what it is not, and to hate indirectly the Cause from which all perfection and all love derive.

This explains why we must both love ourselves and love others; it is because we exist, and are therefore willed by the cause, and it is the Cause which we must love in ourselves and in every creature; our existence is the love that God evinces to us a priori.[1] To love God in ourselves is to eliminate all that separates us from the Cause; to love God in one's neighbor is to treat the latter as we would wish to be treated ourselves with God in view, and not to treat him as we would not deserve to be treated in his place.[2] Since it is impossible that we do to others as much good as we can do to ourselves — sanctity being incommunicable — it would be senseless to love others more than ourselves; a love which does not answer to any objective reality is an empty thing, bound to go astray.[3] The fact that the most precious treasures, the search for which God imposes on us by our very existence, are incommunicable in their saving essence,

1. In Saint John's Gospel, Christ's teaching is set forth with a highly important complementary shade of meaning: "This is my commandment, That ye love one another, as I have loved you" (John 15:12). The text of Saint Matthew states in more detail: "Love your enemies, bless them that curse you, do good to them that hate you, and pray for them which despitefully use you, and persecute you; that ye may be the children of your Father which is in heaven: for he maketh his sun to rise on the evil and on the good, and sendeth rain on the just and on the unjust. For if ye love them which love you, what reward have ye? do not even the publicans the same? . . . Be ye therefore perfect, even as your Father which is in heaven is perfect" (Matt. 5: 44-48). We quote these words at length because they open up fundamental perspectives on the cosmic "dimensions" of charity.

2. The judge who condemns a criminal considers that he would himself deserve the punishment if he had committed the crime. It is absurd to want to abolish the death penalty — a measure of charity in regard to the collectivity! — on the grounds that one would not like to be in the condemned man's place; to be in the place of the condemned man is at the same time to be the murderer; if the condemned man can earn our sympathy it is precisely by being able to recognize his crime and by desiring to pay for it with his life, thereby removing all antagonism between him and us.

3. In maternal love it is the species which is the real subject: it is "sacred egoism," the instinct for preserving the species which through the maternal instinct is eventually capable of sacrificing the mother to the child. But we are speaking, in this chapter, of spiritual, that is principial and permanent, charity and not of accidental heroism.

indicates the limits of charity towards others; disproportionate charity is either passional attachment or hypocrisy. It is not charity to squander ourselves without discrimination, for that would be to render very ill service to our neighbor, since in order to be able to give, it is necessary to be; likewise, humility does not consist in putting our trust in creatures, for to overesteem men, as do the young, is to be unjust towards others and cruel towards oneself. Spiritually, the rights of charity can reach as far as the love of God and the collective interest regulated by the divine Law allow, but rights must never be confused with duties: Saint Francis of Assisi had the right to embrace lepers; he was not obliged to do so, otherwise all the saints would have done the same.

This perspective makes clear why we must also love our enemies: it is because they exist, a fact which proves that God loves them a priori; moreover, their enmity may be no more than accidental, and in that case it could be that they are better men than we and that God loves them more than us. We are perhaps not capable of judging them, although, from another angle, charity never frees us from discriminating between truth and error, in cases where this alternative presents itself; but even when our intelligence, God's gift, allows us to recognize that we are right and others are wrong — or rather when it forces us to recognize this whether we want to or not — we cannot escape the law of love, that is to say, we must in all circumstances unite with the love which is there, which pre-exists, which has created and sustains us — *l'amor che muove il sole e l'altre stelle* (Dante, *Paradiso)* — and which embraces everything which coexists with us. The doctrine of Christ, which places the mystery of charity at the center of spiritual life, is contained in these words: to love one's neighbor as oneself, and to love him as God loves the Creation (His manifestation) in order to share in this universal love, and in consequence: to love him who hates us, because the divine Love embraces all creation, and because it is necessary to rise above the illusory scission between "me" and "the other." With God, love is blessed self-affirmation: within Himself by Beatitude, and "outside" Himself by the Creation; the latter is like the outpouring of the divine Beatitude into nothingness. God is Love, in His Life and in His Act.

*

* *

Nothing can really be opposed to God, for nothing can be outside Being, except Beyond-Being which embraces Being as space envelops the sun; to say that nothing is opposable to Being signifies that "nothingness" is opposable to It, for nothingness alone is not — or does not exist — in any way, but that is precisely why this opposition has no effective existence. However, since nothing is outside God, save nothingness, which is not — and because it is not — this nothingness or this absence of God can be said in some way to play the part of "neighbor" or of "enemy" in regard to God, who is All-Reality. Now the extrinsic charity of God consists a priori in His "putting Himself in the place" of nothingness, that is of unreality or of impossibility, and He does so in creating the world, which is none other than nothingness to which God has lent a particle of His Being. Nothingness is not in any way, as we have said; it is neither real nor possible, and that is why All-Possibility wishes to give existence to it; the world is nothingness become real, or God become unreal, if one can so put it. Since nothingness is not, it is the world which is "neighbor" to God in its stead; it is for the Creation that God "dies" the "death of love," not in Himself, for He is immutable and impassible, but within the cosmos. Every Revelation, let us add, is a kind of death of Light in darkness; everywhere, "the light shineth in darkness; and the darkness comprehended it not" (John 1:5).

"God is Love": this quality of love calls for that of goodness. The goodness of God is the manifestation of His love within His creation; it is the "personal Will," that is to say the Will directed to facts; God personifies Himself for the world, in relation to the world or in terms of the receptacle, and this personification is goodness because the Essence which it personifies admits of no limitations, and thus of nothing which might be contrary to intrinsic goodness.[4] Rigor — or justice — in no way contradicts this: it answers to the refusal of the receptacle to receive goodness, and this refusal, like every evil, is the trace of nothingness in Existence; it comes of the distance which separates the effect from the Cause, or the world from God. This distance is an indirect consequence of a mysterious aspect of the divine Infinity: it is the All realizing nothingness; but once again, it is not a question here of the "personal Will" of God, for that is asserted only in relation to that manifestation of the Essence which is the world. In other terms, Love-Beatitude, which is the Essence of Goodness, is sufficient unto itself; but Goodness, that is to say Love as applied to creatures, calls for Justice; it cannot be without this complement, the cause of which is in relativity itself.[5] All this is doubtless rather haltingly expressed, yet it was indispensable to take at least a summary glance here at the metaphysics of charity.

In the same order of ideas, we would draw attention to the following: it is absurd to reproach the world with imper-

4. It is when speaking of the Essence, not of the Personification, that Meister Eckhart declares: "God is neither good, nor better, nor best *(non est bonus neque melior neque optimus);* if I call God good, it is as if I called black what is white." The Essence is beyond every determination, even of a positive kind; it is "non-goodness" without being badness, "non-being" without being nothingness.

5. According to the doctrine of Islam, God is Beatitude (or Love) "before" creation, and He is Mercy (or Goodness) "since" creation; for the blessed Essence *(Raḥmān),* evil does not exist, since nothing is outside God, whereas for the Act of Mercy *(Raḥīm),* evil has its cause in the receptacle — the *materia prima* — which "provokes" this Act or this "Personification." In any case, the Islamic doctrine does not hesitate to attribute the "creation" of evil to God, in the sense that God is the ontological cause of everything possible, and not insofar as He is "good" a posteriori; it is not possible to admit two final causes, one for "good"

fection while at the same time admitting the world's very existence and to ask oneself why injustices and sufferings exist, for to say "exist" is to say "to be separated from God," hence from Perfection; to say "effect" is to say "distance from the Cause," so that Existence must imply imperfection with a strictly mathematical rigor. A painful separation, for example, is already prefigured in the purely spatial distinction between bodies, which in itself is in no way distressing; it is illogical, in the final analysis, to admit spatial distinction and at the same time to be surprised at the possibility of a moral separation. The root of all evil, we repeat, is the ontological distance between the world and God, a distance which cannot but exist since God is infinite; it has repercussions in all the orders of Existence.[6]

*

* *

How can the divine Goodness be called "infinite" when God is at the same time infinitely just and when moreover the world shows us facts incompatible with an infinity of goodness allied to an infinity of power? But the epithet "infinite" is here metaphysically unsuitable, although it may be legitimate in a certain relative respect: it is appro-

and the other for "evil." God is the direct cause of all good; He is not the direct cause of evil, that is to say He is not the cause of evil as such, but He is the cause of this necessary element of cosmic equilibrium which, in our world and for us, appears as an "evil." The denial of "evil" by Sufis has no other meaning than this.

6. "Idealists" of every kind think it original to deny the inevitable character of human evils, as if they were the first to discover that evils are evils; instead of fighting evil by example and by sanctity, they destroy the good of which evil is the negation; they fight one evil with another and greater evil which for them takes on the appearance of an "angel of light." Unworthy priests, for example, are an unavoidable evil in a religious community counting millions of adherents; but religion is not cured by suppressing it, that is to say by suppressing the priesthood. The saints have not reformed religious orders by destroying their foundations, but by purifying them through their own perfection.

priate, rigorously speaking, only to God as such, as Essence, and not to His qualities, for these limit one another mutually by the very fact of their "coexistence"; seen from this angle, Goodness could not be infinite, since Justice limits it, and conversely; moreover there cannot be two or more infinitudes. However, one can conceive "relative infinitudes," exactly as one can speak of a "relatively absolute": if space is infinite — which is metaphysically inaccurate, since space, being limited by other conditions of existence, cannot be infinite in the absolute sense of the word — if space then is "infinite" in the sense that it is empirically limitless, a straight line could not be called "infinite" in the same sense, although it too has no limit in the dimension which characterizes it; but just as one can say that the geometrical straight line is limitless without being space, one can likewise qualify as infinite a divine quality, such as Goodness, which amounts to saying that a divine quality is like a dimension of God, but that His Being or His Essence goes beyond it. Human goodness is like an arc — a section of a curve — which is limited since it is not the circle; but the divine Goodness is like the limitless straight line, that is to say it is infinite in relation to the human curve, without being infinite in the absolute sense, that is to say in relation to divine Being — or to Beyond-Being represented in our geometrical symbolism by total space. All this amounts to saying, first, that in order to benefit from the infinity of the divine Goodness, man must put himself in harmony with this dimension, in itself unlimited, and secondly, that beings benefit naturally from the divine Goodness to the extent that they are in accord with it existentially.

Goodness by its nature wills every good, just as power, by its nature, is capable of everything; but qualities have their perfection, their fullness and their completion in their being, not in their manifestations, so that it is absurd to insist that we should find in the world the total fulfillment of a divine quality; a manifestation cannot be absolute or infinite without involving a contradiction. The world being manifestation and not Principle, it can comprise on God's part only manifestations, therefore relativities and not principial plenitudes. But the principles of these manifestations are infinite, and this infinity allows the principles to intervene at every point of the cosmic order; they cannot however intervene in a total manner, that is to say to the extent of abolishing the manifested plane and ceasing to be manifestations, for that would be to reduce the world to God, the creation to the Creator, the effect to the Cause. Consequently, to say that God is "infinitely good" signifies not that this Goodness must intervene always and everywhere — a contradictory supposition, as we have seen — but that it is an aspect of the Absolute and that, by this fact, it is in the essence of Existence itself, and can be actualized in a manner either natural or miraculous, according to what the sovereign Possibility requires; in miracles the divine qualities unveil their intrinsic infinity.

If theologians have for centuries been able to speak of the "infinite Goodness" of God, it is because men have still had an adequate intuition of divine Reality, an intuition which has been artificially paralyzed subsequently by means of a perfectly sterile and "unreal" rationalism. And that is why this difficulty is more actual than ever: namely that the miseries of the world seem to mean that God could not be at the same time infinitely good and infinitely powerful, which is to say that He is either infinitely good but impotent, or all-powerful but evil[7]; now, Omnipotence is "limited" extrinsically — or "dimensionally" — at once by Goodness and by Justice, exactly as these two qualities limit one another, as we have already sought to explain. Omnipotence cannot will the absurd; it cannot deny, even on a minute scale and despite all the play of antinomies, a necessary affirmation of Infinitude, nor can it contrive that what cannot but be should not be.

---

7. Saint Augustine refers to this dilemma in his *Confessions*.

*

* *

Fear is the complement of charity: one cannot love God without fearing Him, any more than one can love one's neighbor without respecting him; not to fear God is to prevent Him showing mercy. As for charity towards a man worthy of contempt, it implies, not respect for a creature one cannot respect, but fear of his Creator, who in a certain way stands behind every creature; every man is "made in the image of God" and thus carries the divine imprint. It is this imprint which must be respected in others as in oneself; if love of one's neighbor presupposes love of oneself, respect for one's neighbor presupposes respect for oneself. God's love for His creature is without fear because there is nothing God could fear, as nothing could exist outside Him, that is, outside Being, whence all existence derives; but man's love for God, or even simply for his neighbor, includes fear — or a kind of fear — by reason of the distance which separates this love from its infinite[8] prototype. That which is "fear" in human love will be "rigor" in divine love, for here there is an inverse relationship — and not analogy as in the case of love — for God cannot fear man, and man cannot judge God. Rigor and fear are, moreover, combined on the human plane in the case of paternal or maternal love: a child cannot be rightly brought up without inspiring respect in him and without showing him respect at the same time; to respect him is to "fear" his personality, which we have not created and which may elude us.

To fear God is first of all to see, on the level of action, consequences in causes, sanction in sin, suffering in error; to love God is first to choose God, that is to say, to prefer what brings one nearer Him over what estranges from Him.

8. "Infinite" in relation to the world, for the Infinite in itself is above all quality or determination.

To love God is also to see the divine Cause in its effects, to see God everywhere, in diverse degrees and in various respects; to fear God is also to flee the world, to take refuge in God. There is, in fear as in love, a contemplative aspect and a volitional aspect: the first is a vision and the second a movement, an act. The most immediate aspect of fear — from the point of view of experience — is discernment of the pernicious results in the very causes of our actions; and the most immediate aspect of charity is the choice of the "divine side" in our life. Or again: to love God is to love what brings us nearer to Him; it is to see the divine Cause in the creaturely effect, and at the same time, by compensation, to see the hallmark of nothingness in things; it is to keep oneself in grace. And to fear God is to fear that which takes us away from Him; it is to see the sanction in the sin, and at the same time, by compensation, the reward in a good work; it is to flee the world, even while living among people. Love derives from a contemplative rather than a volitional point of view and from a symbolism that is in a sense "spatial"; fear on the other hand derives from a point of view that is more volitional than contemplative and from a symbolism that is "temporal"; its perspective is necessarily far closer to individual limitations than is that of love. Love greatly excels fear, for "God is Love."

*

* *

Charity should be envisaged in four different relationships: God, man, the individual and the collectivity. There are first two principal relationships, God and man; then, on man's level, the individual and society.

Love of God, which is the very substance of our being, implies love for one's neighbor in the double respect of the individual and the collectivity, which means on the one hand that we cannot love God while hating our neighbor, and on the other that love of one's neighbor in the singular must accord with love of the collective neighbor and conversely, as circumstances may require. And this is vital: if love of God implies, in a contingent manner and by way of consequence, love of one's neighbor — the love of the Sovereign Good containing all charity as the cause contains the effect — love of one's neighbor will presuppose in a quasi-absolute manner the love of God, otherwise it is passional, or materialistic and egoistic at root. Love of God cannot defraud creatures: we may forget men in loving God without thereby lacking charity towards them, but we cannot, without defrauding both men and ourselves, forget God while loving men.

We must here reply to the following question: when we say that love of one's neighbor has its foundation and sufficient reason in love of God, must this be taken to mean that the charity of an atheist — or of an agnostic — is entirely barren of meaning and value? We do not think so, first because love of the neighbor is always, whether one wishes it or not, an indirect love of God, and secondly because the act of charity has its own value and its immediate efficacy; someone about to drown does not ask whether the man who pulls him out believes in God or not. However, the good that an impious man may do is slight compared with the harm he does to himself as well as to others by his convictions and by his way of acting which expresses them; besides, there are actions which are good only on their own level and not in their intention; there is a zeal of pride or of bitterness which kills the soul. Many atheists are charitable merely to show — if only to themselves in their heart of hearts — that they are better than God; likewise, many believers do good works to make a show of their virtue, if only to themselves, instead of telling themselves that in every apparently meritorious act it is God who acts in us. This whole problem of virtue without faith is, by the way, a favorite theme of modern impiety, and with reason, since it is a question of emptying religion of its values by demonstrating that these are to be found outside it.

Man is "made in the image of God"; now he who loves the Principle thereby loves the manifestation of the Principle; he who loves the Cause, loves the effect or the image, not in itself but by virtue of the Cause. However, it may sometimes appear that love of God could prompt us not to love His creatures, and this appearance is moreover inevitable since the difference between the two loves exists, otherwise we could not distinguish between them even verbally: Christ enjoined His disciples to "hate father and mother"[9] in order to follow Him. The difference exists in that the two loves may, by their respective objectives, be incompatible, though this incompatibility lies not in charity as such, far from it, but only in its levels; indeed, when someone appears not to love man because he loves God, this apparent lack of charity is nonetheless a form of charity towards the creature — on a higher level and through God — so that he who hates his "parents" for God's sake loves them thereby in a new way. The worldly confusion between charity and natural — or passional — attachment does not concern the contemplative, whose sanctity is infinitely more profitable to men than would be his complicity in their dissipation. One of the characteristic features of the worldly is that they do not like being lost alone: for them charity means to have their perdition shared by others.

Love for God is higher than love for man; in a distantly analogous way, love for the collectivity takes precedence over love for the individual. The collective interest comes before individual interest if both interests are of the same order, or if the parties concerned are qualitatively equivalent; this means that the collectivity must be of the same quality as the individual either by the fact of its totality, or

9. Voltaire is particularly odious when he seeks to replace this Gospel commandment, of which he understands not the first word, by the contrary opinion, namely that man ought to love his family and even "tenderly" so; hatred of the supernatural here clothes itself in a sentimentality which is at once mawkish and insolent.

by reason of a specific quality, a caste for example; in no case does the purely quantitative collectivity come before the qualitative individual. Love of God comes before love of the neighbor just as the Absolute comes before the relative; likewise, if the interest of society comes before that of the individual, it is because the totality comes before the part and not inversely; the spiritual comes before the temporal, the essential before the accidental and so on. To make oneself useful to society has meaning only on condition that society itself be useful, and it is so only provided it be organized with a view to man's final ends, otherwise it is not even fully human; this means that the value of society, like that of man, is strictly conditional; God alone suffices to Himself. Let us add that materialist and utilitarian egalitarianism comes up against a series of contradictions: for example, if men are equal because they have the same material needs, why are animals, which also have these needs, not the equals of men? One thing is certain, and that is that when man is bad, he is the most harmful and most useless of animals.[10]

If love of God did not take precedence over love for creatures, every passional attachment to something belonging to this world would have a spiritual value; now the creature, imperfect by definition, can never deserve the total love deserved and demanded by perfection. From a certain point of view, sanctity is the adequation between our will and its divine object, an adequation that is never more than approximate in view of the incommensurability of the respective terms; on the other hand it is illogical, for example, to love youth as if it were eternal, or friendship as if it were absolute. We cannot lay too much stress on this: the

10. Humanitarians forget to ask themselves what man is, and what becomes of him when he is cut off from the Transcendent, which is his reason for being. If Rousseau and other "idealists" had foreseen all the outcomes of their inane philanthropy they would have become Carthusian monks.

world is not God, therefore it is separate from Him: this separation appears, within the world, as the imperfection and fragility of all things; everything here below bears the mark of the distance which separates us from the Infinite. In other words: if God is Love, the world cannot be so by the same right; what limits the possibility — or the legitimacy, according to circumstances — of love in the world is precisely the remoteness of the world from its divine Cause; hence charity towards the neighbor could not, without contradiction, be limitless.[11]

In an analogous way, if love of the collectivity — and we have always in view a collectivity "qualified" by tradition — had not higher claims than love of the individual as such, there could be no question of social order, of legal sanctions, of holy war; nothing would protect the individual against other individuals; society would be at the mercy of malefactors and enemies.[12] Society, as we have said, is superior to the individual, just as the whole is superior to the part, or as the tradition — with which society is in a certain

11. The Moslem "loves him who loves God and hates him who hates God" (*ḥadīth*) and who, therefore, is hated by God, since divine hatred leads to damnation. The Christian, for his part, must love his enemies, inasmuch as they are loved by God, and they are so loved because every man has the possibility of salvation and God "sendeth rain on the just and on the unjust." The Christian loves that which, in man, is capable of loving God, and that is why his charity does not extend expressly to animals, and still less to the damned, contrary to what happens in Buddhism. Buddhist charity is a participation in the divine or more exactly the "nirvanic" Charity and is founded, as regards its object, on the capacity of beings to suffer; the normal nourishment of the Buddhist is vegetable, since plants do not suffer; nevertheless, charity extends even to plants in the sense that a man of goodwill would not think of causing them to perish without necessity, any more than he would make an animal suffer uselessly and this applies to all men, whatever may be their traditional perspective.

12. It is an error to think that there exist "pacifist" religions; Buddhism and the Confucian-Taoist tradition are "pacific," but this is quite different.

way identified — is superior to the individual fact; society comes before the individual, if need be, as the norm comes before the exception, not as quantity crushes quality — which implies, precisely, that society should be organized with a view to man's spiritual welfare. The collectivity, as compared with the individual, is like a new being: an individual may suffer harm without reacting, or even let himself be killed without defending himself; that is his spiritual right, unless his function in the collectivity forbids him; but a collectivity cannot behave like an individual — as many kinds of heresy would have it — for it has values to preserve and defend; it has no right to let them perish. This means that charity is determined by truth, that it is valid only in terms of truth: and truth, whether one likes it or not, is on the side of the "law of the jungle" when it is a question of collective man, and to the extent — always relative — that this is the issue; no virtue could abolish the imperative data of collective nature, for the simple reason that this nature is linked to the fatality of physical laws.

In the same way again, if the spiritual were not superior to the temporal, there would never be room for charity of the spirit, since there are always enough material miseries to relieve; material benefit would always have priority over the spiritual and would even render it illegitimate, in contradiction to Christ's reply to the tempter: "Man shall not live by bread alone, but by every word that proceedeth out of the mouth of God"; our ancestors would never have had the moral right to build cathedrals, and Saint Thomas Aquinas would have had to spend his life in feeding the poor or caring for the sick; the question of vocation would not even arise. In this order of ideas, we would add that it is plausible that good works in relation to "infidels" should be first of all missionary activity, thus preaching the faith, and that the exercise of material charity should a priori be based on a common faith giving a meaning to life; but it is obvious that this principle, which is in the logic of things, in no way abolishes the demands of unconditional charity, according to circumstances; the first point of view is that of the collectivity, and the second that of the individual.

Finally, if the essential did not come before the accidental, there would be no sense of proportion to observe in charity, and things of importance would be sacrificed to accessory elements; charity would not go further than the requirements — or the pleasures — of the moment, and it would not even be possible to give a sick man a bitter medicine. This image of bitter medicine shows us an essential but paradoxical aspect of true charity; "For whom the Lord loveth he correcteth; even as a father the son in whom he delighteth" (Prov. 3:12).

*

* *

However, the hierarchical relationships just described are sometimes hidden under contrary appearances, according to circumstances, for the world is made of mirrors which reflect their respective opposites without losing their own qualities; the cosmic play of possibilities, which are innumerable, tends towards "the exception which proves the rule." Thus when love of God is affirmed in only a secondary manner, liturgically for example, love of the neighbor will take precedence over this mode through the importance of the charity to be exercised, for it is better to help an unfortunate person than to sing a hymn — provided one is faced with the alternative in concrete form, otherwise one could never sing; but in that case, it is God who will so to speak occupy the place of the neighbor, according to the words: "For I was an hungered, and ye gave me meat. . . . Inasmuch as ye have done it unto one of the least of these my brethren, ye have done it unto me"[13]

13. It is doubtless to this teaching that Ruysbroek is referring when he considers that it is necessary "to come out of ecstasy in order to give soup

(Matt. 25:35, 40). A love which appears to take legitimate precedence over an act of love for God will in reality always be a love for God, according to the divine Will itself, and thus the normal relationship remains undisturbed.

Likewise — but much more commonly and in a more direct sense — there are circumstances when the particular "neighbor" has precedence over the collective "neighbor," and we have already referred to this possibility: the collectivity has priority over the individual only insofar as it constitutes totality in relation to the latter, but not in the opposite case when the individual, instead of constituting a part, represents on the contrary the principle or quality of the collectivity which is then no more than mere fact, therefore contingency, even quantity. The practical question which arises from the point of view of charity is that of knowing to what extent the interest of the collectivity has priority over that of the individual — or of a particular individual — and conversely; the answer is that charity towards the individual is required when it does not harm the interest of society, nor any higher interest. The charity that society shows towards the monarch is in the interest of the royal function and therefore also in that of the people; the opposite case is that of the prisoner treated with clemency or the condemned man reprieved for exceptional reasons, but not in a purely arbitrary fashion:[14] in this case,

to a beggar"; this opinion is none theless excessive, given that contemplation has priority over action and so possesses a fortiori the value of alms. One must not forget, in fact, this other saying of Christ's: "For ye have the poor always with you; but me ye have not always." This saying — or the incident which it closes — constitutes moreover the rejection, in anticipation, of a utilitarian, quantitative and demagogic moralism which modern men, whether they have faith or not, too readily confuse with Christianity; let us also recall the story of Martha and Mary, where the superiority of contemplation over action — or love of God over love of creatures — is stated in the most formal manner.

14. According to a *ḥadīth*, "the believer can, just once in his life, place pity above duty." According to another, "if you wish God to pardon your

charity is not directly useful to the collectivity, but it arises because it is in the nature of things and does no harm to the common interest; it will therefore have its indirect usefulness, because existence is woven not only of necessity, but also of liberty. The excellence of the monarch resides in the fact that he represents in an active and conscious manner what is qualitative in the collectivity, namely its traditional heritage in the broadest sense, or more precisely the spiritual heritage when the monarch is also a pontiff; this character extends even to inanimate things, such as objects of sacred art, which

sin and to cover it, you too must cover people's sins; for once the sinner has been brought before the monarch, punishment must be carried out." In the case of the adulterous woman saved by Christ from the hands of the judges, the two perspectives clash: on the one hand that of the collectivity, in principle qualitative — because determined by religious Law — and acting as impersonal norm and divine instrument with respect to an individual in contempt of the Law and threatening the social equilibrium, and on the other hand that of the individual considered in herself, outside any question of opportuneness, in her inner freedom and her capacity for spiritual transmutation. From the Mosaic point of view, the sinful woman was as it were the incarnation of disequilibrium and revolt, and stoning was a kind of magical action; the stones symbolized the implacability of the divine norm, the collectivity which hurls them representing the impersonal, anonymous and universal character of the Law. Let us add that Christ saved the adulterous woman not only in the name of a supra-social perspective taking account of the intrinsic value of the individual, but also by reason of the unworthiness of the crowd, which had become unfit to perform the impersonal function of "social magic"; in other respects, Christ's intervention has a certain analogy with that of the Angel in Abraham's sacrifice. The Mosaic ordinance to stone even an ox and not to eat its flesh afterwards proves that the ox was killed as a "scapegoat" of an impersonal, one could say "cosmic," evil, and that stoning was a "magical" not a moral practice. Many cruel practices were aimed principally at neutralizing the root of an evil through its manifestation and thus "dissolving" certain possibilities of disequilibrium; this is a case of applying the principle of the "lesser evil," which must be accepted for a given environment and concerning which no doubts can be admitted without casting doubt on Revelation itself.

111

by virtue of their sometimes highly important and even in fact irreplaceable spiritual function, can take precedence over temporal needs.[15]

The interest of the living being — individual or collective — sometimes requires suffering: thus the carnivores are useful because they eliminate feeble individuals from among the animals on which they prey and so prevent degeneration of these species; in the case of man, as long as weapons had not yet become machines of quantitative destruction, tribal or feudal warfare played an analogous part, not to mention epidemics and other scourges which, it must be said, are indispensable to collectivities;[16] moreover, account must be taken of the conditions of this "iron age," in which collectivities are particularly subject to the passions and exposed to every kind of corruption. The individual possesses a will of his own, he

15. It is sometimes said that a monarch or a pontiff ought to live in every respect like a poor man, but this is again to confuse the particular and the collective. The man who rules is like an incarnation of the collectivity; the psychological pressure which surrounds him is such — from the point of view of responsibility and also by the simple fact of the presence of an immense collective periphery — that he has a genuine need of his palaces, gardens and servants, of which he is in any case more or less a prisoner. Likewise, if a bishop wears pontifical vestments, and not the simple garb of the Apostles, this is not because he lacks simplicity, but on the contrary because, being neither an Apostle nor Christ, he must reflect their glory before the collectivity and assume something of the honor which is their due; in this respect, sacerdotal — or royal — insignia are strictly necessary. A Prophet, a saint, or a nomad chief can share the life of the poorest in every respect; but the spiritual and temporal authorities governing the great sedentary peoples are obliged to isolate themselves in a pageantry without which the character of their position would be forgotten; this pageantry is moreover for the people a factor of strength and of faith, because it externalizes the greatness and continuity of the nation and reflects the proximity of Heaven.

16. It is not possible, logically, to call a morality "humanitarian" when it eliminates partial evils at the expense of the patient's life, but this is basically the nature of all modern progressivist tendencies.

can give it a particular direction and thus defeat the agents of corruption which our nature includes; but the collectivity — in the most general sense — is passive and unconscious, its will is undetermined and multiple, it possesses no principle of intellectual or moral homogeneity, and this shows the error of humanitarianism which seeks to treat the collectivity as a homogeneous being, and even an essentially good and lucid being.[17]

*

* *

We have seen that the principal injunctions of charity combine in different ways, according to the particular case; the higher interest can neutralize the lower, and this gives rise to seeming paradoxes which a superficial moralism enjoys stigmatizing. "Idealists" are prone to form judgements based on a fragmentary aspect, which they have every interest in isolating from the total order; having no idea of the ineluctable, nor of the "lesser evil," nor of the law of compensations, they do not hesitate to compromise a great good — the scope of which is beyond their grasp — for a petty advantage, which strikes their imagination all the more strongly since they do not know how relative it is. To say that true charity is universal means, not that it abolishes barriers which are natural

17. The same mistake is met with in the many "idealists" who demand from a whole traditional collectivity — that is to say one embracing whole peoples — the saintliness of "apostolic times," as if a latter-day and countless community ought still to possess a general perfection which only a small group was able to realize, all impregnated as it was by the historical closeness to the Word. And without being able themselves to show the least trace of sanctity, these people pass over, in hypocritical silence, the saints who have perpetuated this perfection of the original times down to our own days; this is made all the more easy by the abolition of the very notion of sanctity and its replacement by a kind of hollow and inoperative "sincerity."

and therefore broadly speaking unavoidable, but that it has its place in all realms and on all levels.[18]

Despite the inspired commentaries bequeathed to us by tradition as well as the example of many saints, it could be objected here that Christ's commandment to love our enemies, to do good to those who hate us and to offer the left cheek to those who smite us on the right, has an unconditional character and that more subtle interpretations, which take account of the differences between an individual and his function, or between the individual and society, are to be explained only by weakness or the sinful nature of men. Now the Gospel commandments in question can be understood only by grasping their particular and underlying intention, as, for example, in the case of the following

18. To feed on animals cannot be considered as a transgression — except in the case of traditional injunctions forbidding flesh as food, or attaching to a particular animal either a sacred character or a character of impurity — but the blood that is spilt should be offered to the Divinity so that the animal's soul "does not bring a complaint before the Creator" and does not, in revenge, provoke the spilling of human blood. We are here alluding to a Mazdeist conception, according to which a quasi-angelic personification of the ox's soul brings a complaint before the Divinity about the outrages that men inflict on cattle. Judeo-Moslem sacrifices and other rites of this kind, certain hunting rites for example, reconcile the genius of the species with man, who thus assumes with respect to the animal the function of "pontiff" (*pontifex*), in the etymological sense of the word. It is true that monotheist perspectives have no awareness of this aspect of the rites in question, because consideration of the animal soul lies outside the framework of their doctrines. However that may be, their charity does sometimes extend to animals: "Fear God — says a *ḥadīth* — in your treatment of dumb animals; mount them when they are fit to carry you, and dismount when they are tired." To the question as to whether there are "rewards for our good actions to quadrupeds," the Prophet replied: "In truth, there are rewards in Heaven for every act of charity to an animal." The argument that a plant is also a living being and that, consequently, vegetarianism arbitrarily stops half-way, is not acceptable, for it is not the fact of being alive which matters here but the capacity of animals to suffer, as also a certain "impurity" of meat, and above all of blood.

saying, disconcerting as is its literal meaning: "for all they that take the sword shall perish with the sword" (Matt. 26:52); this is a principial affirmation of the law of "concordant actions and reactions," a law which concerns us insofar as our acts are the expression of an individual and passional will — but in this case the "sword" which causes us to perish can have very diverse forms, posthumous as well as terrestrial. The commandments quoted above are not fully explainable unless the following is taken into account: to arrive at God, we have to surmount, at its most sensitive point, the egocentric illusion which is at the basis of all evils; the question of knowing whether or not we are right in regard to the enemy is of no interest here, since we are all sinners and injustice is deserved a priori. This perspective obviously concerns the individual as a spiritual entity, not as an impersonal instrument of the collectivity, which amounts to saying that it concerns the particular individual and not the social collectivity, at least not directly; finally this charity concerns the enemy as regards his hatred for us personally rather than his hatred for God, as is shown by Christ's violence towards the moneychangers in the Temple. It is true that there is not always, in practice, a sharp dividing line between the two points of view, but it is then for the individual, for his conscience, for inspiration, to put the emphasis where it ought to be. In any case, to give to Christ's spiritual commandments a unilateral and altogether outward meaning would impose on the Church — or the Churches — the most fatal of hypocrisies and condemn them purely and simply to disappearance.[19]

---

19. Let us mention here that the Koran while on the one hand admitting the law of retaliation for cases of intentional murder, on the other hand praises "those who overcome evil with good"; there is no contradiction here since this commandment, according to the commnentators, is not valid except for cases where the good can effectively "overcome" evil; nor moreover did Christ, when He enjoined the offering of the other cheek, mean that in the case of murder it was necessary to offer a new victim, or that in the case of the sacking of a town, another town had to

We would give further precision to our thoughts as follows: Christ could not have failed to know that His religion would one day embrace the whole Empire, and that an Empire — or a State — is not an individual; that, consequently, the Christianization of a total collectivity, of a State, would ipso facto add a new mode to the Gospel morality, a mode based on the concrete nature and the inevitable demands of an entire society, and in principle contained in the very "letter" of the Gospel, thanks to its universality. Such is the meaning, it would seem, of that mysterious passage in Saint Luke's Gospel (Luke 22:35-38): "Lord, behold, here are two swords. And he said unto them, It is enough." The sword that must be bought (verse 36) doubtless represents the constitution of the Christian State; the first of the two swords offered by the Apostles would symbolize the power of judge and justiciary with respect to society, and the second the power of warfare with respect to the enemy.[20] The reality of the Christian State had in fact already been declared in this saying: "Render unto Caesar

be handed over to the enemy. The fact that Jesus tolerated for an instant two of his disciples carrying swords, or Saint Peter carrying one, proves in our eyes the relatively legitimate character — because it is based on the inevitable — of armed defense; it is as if the Apostles had carried these swords, not for themselves, but for the Christian empire of the future, the State which was to be heir to Caesar.

20. To contest such an interpretation in the name of charity is to admit by implication that Christ had wished, for Christianity, anarchy within and destruction from without. Obviously, the two swords can have yet other meanings; they can refer, in particular, to royalty and to the Empire respectively, the latter concerning Christianity and the former the peoples who constitute it. Pope Boniface VIII in his bull *Unam Sanctam* sees in the two swords the temporal and spiritual powers; other commentators have given the same opinion. Let us recall here that according to Saint Thomas, "since the literal meaning is that which is intended by the author, and since the author of the Holy Scriptures is God whose Intellect grasps all things simultaneously, there is nothing improper — as Saint Augustine says — in allowing several meanings to follow the literal sense in a given passage of Scripture" *(Summa Theologica, De Deo* I, 10).

that which is Caesar's. . . ."; now the legitimate demands or the vital needs of this new "dimension" — new in relation to the primitive Church — which is the Christian State, could not run contrary to sanctity, as is proven moreover by such examples as Saint Maurice, Saint Louis, Saint Joan of Arc or Saint Alexander Nevsky; the imperfection of social and political functions, in a traditional society, is no more opposed to sanctity than is the body. Or again, if the perfection of the priestly function or of the monastic state does not carry with it a guarantee of spiritual perfection, neither does the imperfection of earthly necessities, in turn, carry with it an obstacle to this perfection; that which is humanly necessary is spiritually neutral, and can for that reason take on a positive aspect.

This leads to the question of knowing what is intrinsically moral and what is not: there are two criteria, the first inward and the second outward, always provided it is agreed, as it must be, that the spiritual has priority over the social. The inward criterion of the moral — or one might say of the non-immoral[21] — is conformity with the fundamental virtues; the outward criterion is conformity with the nature of things. Thus, when one is confronted with unfamiliar customs, with polygamy for example, it is a question of knowing, not whether these customs would be moral or immoral if we practiced them ourselves, such as we are and in the framework of our own life, but rather whether or not they are compatible with the virtues on the one hand and with social realities on the other, that is to say, as regards this latter aspect, whether they reflect a real aspect of human existence and thereby an aspect of ontological truth. It results from this that certain customs are "moral" within one intellectual, cultural and mental framework, but would be "immoral" in another; that alone is immoral in itself

21. In the course of our preceding works, we have had occasion to point out that such a manner of expressing oneself comprises a nuance that is far from being superfluous.

which is contrary to pure truth and to human nature as such. It should never be overlooked in the West that if homicide is compatible with the most supernatural virtues — otherwise, what would become of warrior saints? — there is no reason to believe a priori that polygamy, which after all God did not forbid to the Jews, should by its very nature be incompatible with morality, that is to say, with equilibrium between earth and the Spirit.[22]

Like every virtue, charity is above all a spiritual principle; the assessing of its practical modalities is a matter of perspective and of sentiment; to identify charity with such and such definite actions belongs to morality, but morality cannot take full account of the higher truth of which it is a particular crystallization. The world is so made that we can accomplish nothing without neglecting some possibilities; outward charity is always a choice, never a total gift.

The conclusion is that charity cannot fully define itself except by starting from a revealed spiritual perspective, that is to say from a divinely willed manner of loving God; the rest is a matter of vocation, expediency, sensitivity. Charity,

---

22. Polygamy has its natural root in certain aspects of the physiological inequality of the sexes and also in certain political structures, and its spiritual root in the relationship *Ātmā-Māyā: Ātmā* is in fact unique, while *Māyā* is multiple; monogamy, on the other hand, is founded on the sexual complementarism as such, hence on the relationship Purusha-Prakriti and on the primordial pair. But each of these two points of view includes the other in its own way. The relativity of moral conceptions and of the associations of ideas belonging to them appears in a striking way in the false generalizations of the moralism of dress which has decimated many tribes; people worry about "morals" — with or without ulterior commercial motives — and are incapable of seeing the immoral character of that kind of universal degradation spread with certain forms of clothing. This official and "civilized" moralism seems to prefer the clothed adulterer to virgin nudity; among peoples nude by tradition, it readily has a meaning of pedantry, greed, even maleficence. Let us add here that sacred nudity, in Hinduism, is not unrelated to the purifying quality of the air which, being an element, is simple, and hence incorruptible, a fact that Jains express in prescribing the "wearing of the air as a garment."

from the point of view of vocation, is what God demands of us; the charity of one will be to visit the sick, that of another to teach truth; but, apart from vocation, there is a charity which is imposed on us all, because we are all human beings. The gift of ourselves to God calls down a gift of God to ourselves; by the same token it calls for a gift of ourselves to men, as a sequel to what God has given us. The greatest charity is the gift of that which, at bottom, we have no longer the power to give, because the prime mover of such charity is God.

*

* *

There is in our good works and in our virtues a poison which is eliminated only by the conviction that God has no need of all this, and that they must be given freely like the flowers of the fields. Our actions have importance to the extent that they determine something in ourselves and in our surroundings, two realms subject to the divine norms; but what God wants of us — while wanting nothing of course — is our soul, our vital center, the ego, and through it our immortal personality. In the final analysis, God wants Himself in us. One must therefore beware of any materialistic and demagogic conception of charity and never forget that what "interests" God — and the sole thing that can interest Him — is the eternal life of him who gives and the eternal life of him who receives.

True charity — we might call it "integral charity" — gives nothing without giving inwardly something better; the art of giving requires that to the material gift should be added a gift of the soul: this is to forget the gift after having given it, and this forgetfulness is like a fresh gift. Intrinsically, that virtue alone is good which is in a certain way unconscious of itself and, as a result, becomes neither "egoistic charity" nor "proud humility." As an old proverb has it, "Do good and throw it into the sea; if the fish swallow it and men forget it, God will remember it."

119

In order to act well, one must be: to be able to give the best, one must know that this best comes only from God. The saints alone dissolve evil at its roots; others merely move it aside. Indeed the charity of the ordinary man is never wholly charitable: what the sinner gives with the right hand, he takes back with the left, or in other words, he removes indirectly what he gives directly, so that his charity is like a gift given by a thief; this, however, is certainly not a reason for him to abstain from giving; but at least he should not boast of it. The first act of charity is to rid the soul of illusions and passions and thus rid the world of a maleficent being; it is to make a void so that God may fill it and, by this fullness, give Himself. A saint is a void open for the passage of God.

Modes of Prayer

The most elementary mode of orison — of contact between man and God — is no doubt prayer in the most ordinary sense of the word, for it is the direct expression of the individual, of his desires and fears, his hopes and gratitude. This prayer is however less perfect than canonical prayer which has a universal character due to the fact that God is its author and that the reciting subject is not a particular individual, but man as such, the human species; also this prayer contains nothing which does not concern man — every man — and this is as much as to say that it includes, eminently or in addition, all possible individual prayers; it can even render them redundant, and in fact, the Revelations permit or recommend individual prayer, but do not impose it. Canonical prayer shows its universality and its timeless value by being very often expressed in the first person plural, and also by its preference for using a sacred or liturgical and therefore symbolically universal language, so that it is impossible for whoever recites it not to pray for all and in all.

As to individual prayer, grounds for its existence are incontestably to be found in our nature, since individuals do in fact differ from one another and have different destinies and desires.[1] The aim of this prayer is not only to

1. With the *Avatāras* every personal prayer becomes polyvalent and canonical, as is shown by the Psalms for example; but these great Messen-

obtain particular favors, but also the purification of the soul: it loosens psychic knots or, in other words, dissolves subconscious coagulations and drains away many secret poisons; it externalizes before God the difficulties, failures and crispations of the soul, which presupposes that the soul be humble and genuine, and this externalization — carried out in the face of the Absolute — has the virtue of reestablishing equilibrium and restoring peace, in a word, of opening us to grace.[2] All this is offered us as well and a fortiori by canonical prayer, but the human spirit is in general too weak to extract from it all the remedies it contains.

The personal character of non-canonical prayer does not imply that it is free from rules, for the human soul — as the Psalms admirably show — is always the same in its miseries and joys, and therefore in its duties towards God; it is not enough for a man to formulate his petition, he must express also his gratitude, resignation, regret, resolution and praise. In his petition, man is looking for some favor, provided it be of a nature agreeable to God, and so to the universal Norm. Thankfulness is the consciousness that every favor of destiny is a grace which might not have been

gers give us at the same time the pattern of spontaneous prayer, since they but rarely repeat the prayers of others, and in any case show us that canonical prayer must be said with spontaneity, as if it were the first or the last prayer of our life.

2. The sacrament of penitence is founded on these data, adding to them a particular compensatory quality of celestial grace. Psychoanalysis offers an analogous process, but in satanic form, for it replaces the supernatural by the infra-natural: in the place of God, it puts the blind, dark and inhuman aspects of nature. For psychoanalysts evil is not what is contrary to God and to the final ends of man, but what troubles the soul, even if the cause of disquiet be beneficial; further, the equilibrium resulting from psychoanalysis is basically of an animal order, and this is entirely contrary to the requirements of our immortality. In man, his disequilibria can and must be resolved with a view to a higher equilibrium, conformable to a spiritual hierarchy of values, and not in some quasi-vegetative state of bliss; a human evil cannot be cured apart from God.

given; and if it is true that man has always something to ask, it is just as true, to say the least, that he always has grounds for gratitude; without this, no prayer is possible. Resignation is the anticipated acceptance of the non-fulfillment of some request; regret or contrition — the asking of pardon — implies consciousness of what puts us in opposition to the divine Will; resolution is the desire to remedy a given transgression, for our weakness must not make us forget that we are free.[3] Finally, praise signifies not only that we relate every value to its ultimate Source, but also that we see every trial in terms of its necessity or its usefulness, or in its aspect of fatality and of grace. If petition is a capital element of prayer, it is because we can do nothing without the help of God; man's resolves offer no guarantee — the example of Saint Peter shows this — if he does not ask for this help.

*

* *

Another mode of orison is meditation; the contact between man and God here becomes contact between the intelligence and Truth, or relative truths contemplated in view of the Absolute. There is a certain outward analogy between meditation and individual prayer in that man formulates his thought spontaneously in both cases; the difference, which is infinitely more important, is that meditation is objective and intellectual — unless it is a question of imaginative, even sentimental reflections, which are not what we have in mind here — whereas prayer is subjective and volitive. In meditation, the aim is knowledge, hence a reality which in principle goes beyond the ego as such; the thinking subject is then, strictly speaking, the impersonal

3. Logically, regret and resolution are inseparable, but a regret can be conceived without resolution, and this is tepidness or despair, as also a resolution without regret, and this is pride, unless it be based on wisdom. It is not a question here primarily of sentimentality, but of attitudes of the will, whether or not these are accompanied by feelings.

intelligence, hence man and God at the same time, pure intelligence being the point of intersection between human reason and the divine Intellect.

Meditation acts on the one hand upon the intelligence, in which it awakens certain consubstantial "memories," and on the other hand upon the subconscious imagination which ends by incorporating in itself the truths meditated upon, resulting in a fundamental and as it were organic process of persuasion. Experience proves that one man can do great things even in unfavorable circumstances, provided that he believes himself capable of accomplishing them, while another, more gifted perhaps, but doubting himself, will do nothing even in favorable conditions; man walks fearlessly on flat ground, but imagination may prevent him taking a single step when he has to pass between two chasms. From this one sees the importance of meditation even simply from the point of view of autosuggestion; in the spiritual life, as in other fields, it is a precious help to be deeply convinced both as to the things towards which we are tending, and also of our capacity to attain them, with the help of God.

Meditation — as defined in the language of the Vedanta — is essentially "investigation" *(vichāra)* leading to the assimilation of theoretical truth, and then discernment *(viveka)* between the Real and the unreal; there are here two levels, one ontological and dualist, and the other centered on Beyond-Being or the Self, and consequently non-dualist; it is the whole difference between *bhakti* and *jnāna*.

Pure concentration also is orison, on condition that it have a traditional basis and be centered on the Divine; this concentration is none other than silence[4] which, indeed,

4. "The Father spoke one word, and this Word was His Son, and this Word He spoke without end in an eternal silence, and it is in this silence that the soul hears it" (Saint John of the Cross: *Spiritual Sentences and Counsels*, 307).

has been called a "Name of the Buddha" because of its connection with the idea of the Void.[5]

*

* *

We have distinguished canonical prayer from individual prayer by saying that in the latter it is a given individual who is the subject, while in the former the subject is man as such; now there is an orison wherein God Himself is in a sense the Subject, and that is the pronouncing of a revealed divine Name.[6] The foundation of this mystery is, on the one hand, that "God and His Name are one" (Ramakrishna), and on the other, that God Himself pronounces His Name in Himself, hence in eternity and outside all creation, so that His unique and uncreate word is the prototype of ejaculatory prayer and even, in a less direct sense, of all orison. The first distinction that the intellect conceives in the Divine Nature is that of Beyond-Being and Being; but since Being is so to speak the "crystallization" of Beyond-Being, it is like the "Word" of the Absolute, through which the latter expresses Itself, determines Itself, or names Itself.[7] Another distinc-

5. *Shunyāmūrti*, "Manifestation of the Void," is one of the Names of the Buddha. The silent prayer of the North American Indians, which presupposes a symbolist outlook and the framework of virgin Nature, offers striking analogies with Zen.

6. In his *Cudgel for Illusion*, Shankara sings: "Control thy soul, restrain thy breathing, distinguish the transitory from the True, repeat the holy Name of God, and thus calm the agitated mind. To this universal rule apply thyself with all thy heart and all thy soul." The connection between metaphysical discrimination and the practice of invocation is one of capital importance. We find the same connection in this *Stanza on the Yellow Robe* (of *sannyāsīs*), also by Shankara: "Singing *Brahma*, the word of Deliverance, meditating uniquely on 'I am *Brahma*,' living on alms and wandering freely, blessed, certainly, is the wearer of the ochre robe."

7. In the Torah, God says to Moses: "I am that I am" *(Eheieh asher Eheieh);* this refers to God as Being, for it is only as Being that God creates, speaks and legislates, since the world exists only in relation to Being. In the Koran, this same utterance is rendered as follows: "I am God" *(Ana*

tion which is essential here and which derives from the preceding by principial succession,[8] is that between God and the world, the Creator and the Creation: just as Being is the Word or Name of Beyond-Being, so too the world — or Existence — is the Utterance of Being, of the personal God; the effect is always the "name" of the cause.[9]

But whereas God, in naming Himself, firstly determines Himself as Being and secondly, starting from Being, manifests Himself as Creation — that is to say that He manifests Himself "within the framework of nothingness" or "outside Himself," and so in illusory mode[10] — man, for his part, when pronouncing the same Name, describes the inverse movement, for this Name is not only Being and Creation, but also Mercy and Redemption; in man, it does not create, but on the contrary "undoes," and that in a divine manner since it brings man back to the Principle.

'Llâh); this means that Being *(Anâ,* "I") derives from Beyond-Being *(Allâh,* this Name designating the Divinity in all Its aspects without any restriction); it is thus that the Koranic formula refers to the divine Prototype of the pronouncing of the Name of God. *Anâ 'Llâh* signifies implicitly that "God and his Name are one" — since Being "is" Beyond-Being inasmuch as it is its "Name" — and for the same reason the Son is God, while not being the Father. What gives its metaphysical force to the Hebraic formula is the return of "being" on itself; and what gives its force to the Arabic formula is the juxtaposition, without copula, of "subject" and "object."

8. By "descent" *(tanazzulah)* as Sufis would say.

9. This relationship is repeated on the plane of Being itself, where it is necessary to distinguish between the Father and the Son — or between Power and Wisdom — the Holy Spirit being intrinsically Beatitude-Love and extrinsically Goodness or Radiation. This is the "horizontal" or ontological perspective of the Trinity; according to the "vertical" or gnostic perspective — ante-Nicene one might say — it would be said that the Holy Spirit proceeds from Beyond-Being as All-Possibility and dwells in Being as the totality of creative possibilities, while radiating forth into Existence, which is in harmony with the concept of creation by love.

10. It is absurd to reproach Creation for not being perfect, that is to say for not being divine, or in other words uncreated. God cannot will that the world be, and at the same time that it should not be the world.

The divine Name is a metaphysical isthmus (in the sense of the Arabic word *barzakh):* as "seen by God," it is determination, limitation, "sacrifice"; as seen by man, it is liberation, limitlessness, plenitude. We have said that this Name, invoked by man, is nonetheless always pronounced by God; human invocation is only the "outward" effect of eternal and "inward" invocation by the Divinity. The same holds true for every other Revelation: it is sacrificial for the divine Spirit and liberating for man; Revelation, whatever its form or mode, is descent or incarnation for the Creator, and ascent or "excarnation" for the creature.[11]

The sufficient reason for the invocation of the Name is the remembering of God; and this, in the final analysis, is not other than consciousness of the Absolute. The Name actualizes this consciousness and, in the end, perpetuates it in the soul and fixes it in the heart, so that it penetrates the whole being and at the same time transmutes and absorbs it. Consciousness of the Absolute is the prerogative of human intelligence, and also its aim.

Or again: we are united to the One by our being, by our pure consciousness and by the symbol. It is by the symbol — the Word — that man, in central and quintessential orison, realizes both Being and Consciousness, the latter in the former and conversely. The perfection of Being, which is Extinction, is prefigured by deep sleep, and also, in other ways, by beauty and virtue; the perfection of Consciousness, which is Identity — or Union, if this term be preferred — is prefigured by concentration, and also, a priori, by intelli-

11. In Japanese Amidic Buddhism, there have been controversies over the question of whether invocations of the Buddha must be innumerable or whether on the contrary one single invocation suffices for salvation, the sole condition being, in both cases, a perfect faith and, as a corollary, abstention from evil, or the sincere intention so to abstain. In the first case, invocation is envisaged from the human side, that is from the standpoint of duration, while in the second case, it is conceived in its principial, hence its divine and therefore timeless reality; *Jodo Shinshu,* as also Hindu *Japa-Yoga,* combines both perspectives.

gence and contemplation. Beauty does not of course produce virtue, but it favors in a certain way a pre-existing
virtue; likewise, intelligence does not produce contemplation, but it broadens or deepens a contemplation that is
natural. Being is passive perfection and Consciousness
active perfection. "I sleep, but my heart waketh."

*
* *

Why is it that Being is "Word" or "Name"[12] rather than
"Thought," "Act" or "Sacrifice," and why is it that ejaculatory prayer also is not thought, act, sacrifice, and so on?
First it is quite true that Being has all these aspects, and
many others as well; these aspects are to be found in every
Revelation. Nonetheless, speech on the one hand realizes
all possible aspects of affirmation, and on the other has a
kind of pre-eminence from the fact that it is the feature
which most notably distinguishes man from animals.
Speech implies thought, since it is an exteriorization, but
thought does not imply speech; analogously, speech, while
itself an act, adds to action a new dimension of intelligibility. Similarly, speech has an aspect of sacrifice in the sense
that it limits what it expresses; and as for ejaculatory prayer
— which being speech, is at the same time thought, act and
sacrifice — it comprises yet another aspect of sacrifice or
asceticism from the fact that it excludes all other preoccupation of the heart and thereby is a "poverty" or a *vacare
Deo*. Or again, man, at the moment of birth, manifests his
voice before any other faculty, and this cry is already —
though doubtless unconsciously — a prayer, as being a

12. Meister Eckhart says in his commentary on the Gospel of Saint
John that "the Father neither sees, nor hears, nor speaks, nor wishes
anything but His own Name. It is by means of His Name that the Father
sees, hears and manifests Himself. The Name contains all things. Essence
of the Divinity, it is the Father Himself. . . . The Father gives thee His
eternal Name, and it is His own life, His being and His divinity that He
gives thee in one single instant by His Name."

prefiguration or a symbol; likewise for the last gasp of the dying man, or his last breath, since voice and breath refer to the same symbolism.

Every normal activity, needless to say, reflects in its way the eternal Act of God: thus a weaver could say that Being is the first divine "fabric," in the sense that Beyond-Being weaves into it the principial possibilities — the "divine Names" — and that Being in its turn weaves the existential manifestations, hence angels, worlds, beings.[13] Not every man, however, is a weaver, but every man speaks, which shows clearly that speech has priority over secondary and more or less "accidental" activities; these are too outward to be assimilable to prayers, but they can be the vehicle of orison by virtue of their symbolical quality.[14] In other words, any kind of occupation, whether a craft or otherwise — provided that it is "natural" — can be a spiritual support not only thanks to the symbolism inherent in it, which would not suffice by itself, but above all by virtue of the contemplative orison superimposed on it, which actualizes the value of the symbol.

*
* *

The principle according to which "prayer of the heart" can replace all other rites — on condition of sufficient spiritual maturity — is to be found in Hesychasm, but is much more emphasized in the Hindu and Buddhist paths, where the abandonment of general ritual prayers and prac-

---

13. It is this second proposition which the artisan will adopt in fact, the first belonging to the province of pure metaphysics, and not necessarily entering into the outlook of craft initiations, which have a cosmological basis.

14. It is thus that one ought to understand every fundamental and naturally "ritual" activity, the gesture of the sower for example, or the work of the mason; is not God He who sows the cosmic possibilities in the *Materia prima* and, in the soul, the truths and graces, and is He not the "Great Architect of the Universe"?

tices is considered normal and sometimes even a *conditio sine qua non*. The profound reason for this is that it is necessary to distinguish between the realm of the "divine Will" and that of the "divine Nature"; the latter "is what it is" and is expressed by the Name alone, whereas the former projects into the human world differentiated — and necessarily relative — wills and is expressed by complex prayers, corresponding to the complexity of human nature.[15] Rites, however — especially those of a purifying or sacramental character — can be considered as necessary aids to support prayer of the heart; this belongs to a point of view deriving from a perspective differing from the one just envisaged, and better suited to certain temperaments.

We would doubtless hesitate to speak of these things if others — Westerners as well as Asians — did not speak of them, and if we were not living at a time when all sorts of testimonies are demanded and when the compensating Mercy simplifies many things, though this cannot mean that everything will become easily accessible. It is obvious that a spiritual means has significance only within the rules assigned to it by the tradition which offers it, whether it is a question of outward or inward rules; nothing is more dangerous than to give oneself up to improvisations in this field. This reservation will not fail to surprise those who hold that man is free in all respects before God, and who will ask by what right we seek to subject prayer to conditions and to enclose it within frameworks. The reply is simple, and it is the Bible itself which gives it: "Thou shalt not take the name of the Lord thy God in vain; for the Lord thy God will not acquit him that takes his name in vain" (Exod. 20:7;

---

15. Herein lies the whole difference between form and essence, which penetrates every domain. If "in the resurrection they neither marry, nor are given in marriage," this relates to mode or form, not to essence; if on the other hand Paradise shelters *houris,* this relates to essence and not to mode; and it is in relation to essence that Saint Bernard could speak of "torrents of voluptuous delight."

Deut. 5:11). Now man is a priori "vain" according to certain spiritual criteria, those precisely which apply when it is a question of direct and "mystagogic" methods; man is thus not absolutely free, apart from the fact that absolute Freedom belongs to God alone. Only that which is given by Him has value for salvation, not that which is taken by man; it is God who has revealed His Names, and it is He who determines their usage; and if, according to the Apostle "whosoever shall eat this (divine) bread unworthily eateth damnation to himself" (1 Cor. 11:27-29), the same holds true for the presumptuous use of ejaculatory prayers.

This being admitted, we can return to the positive side of the question: in whatever degree it may be opportune, according to circumstances and surroundings, ejaculatory prayer results from these two requirements: perfection and continuity. "Pray without ceasing," says the Apostle (1 Thess. 5:17),[16] and "Likewise the Spirit also helpeth our infirmities: for we know not what we should pray for as we

16. Basing himself on the Gospel: "And he spake a parable unto them to this end, that men ought always to pray, and to not faint" (Luke 18:1); "Watch ye therefore, and pray always, that ye may be accounted worthy to escape all these things . . ." (Luke 21:36). Saint Bernardino of Siena says in a sermon that "the name [of Jesus] is origin without origin" and that it is "as worthy of praise as God himself"; and again: "Everything which God has created for the salvation of the world is hidden in this Name of Jesus" (San Bernardino da Siena: *Le Prediche Volgari*). It is not by chance that Bernardino gave to his cypher of the Name of Jesus the appearance of a monstrance: the divine Name, carried in thought and in the heart, through the world and through life, is like the Holy Sacrament carried in procession. This cypher of the Greek letters I H S, signifying *Iesous*, but interpreted in Latin as *In Hoc Signo* or as *Jesus Hominum Salvator* and often written in Gothic letters, can be analyzed in its primitive form into three elements — a vertical straight line, two vertical lines linked together, and a curved line — and thus contains a symbolism at once metaphysical, cosmological and mystical; there is in it a remarkable analogy, not only with the name *Allāh* written in Arabic, which also comprises the three lines of which we have just spoken (in the form of the *alif*, the two *lams* and the *hā*), but also with the Sanskrit monosyllable *Aum*, which is composed of three *mātrās* (A U M) indicating a "rolling up" and

ought: but the Spirit itself maketh intercession for us with groanings which cannot be uttered" (Rom. 8:26).[17]

*

* *

The Divine Names have meanings which are particular because belonging to a revealed language and universal because referring to the supreme Principle. To invoke a Divinity is to enunciate a doctrine: he who says "Jesus," says implicitly that "Christ is God,"[18] which signifies that God "came down" in order that man should be able to "ascend";[19] moreover, to say that "God was made man" signifies at the same time that man is fallen, since the justification for the Divine descent is the fact that man exists "below"; God "takes on flesh" because man is "flesh," and flesh means fall, passion, misery. Christianity takes its starting point in the volitional aspect of man;

thereby a return to the Center. All these symbols mark, in a certain sense, the passage from "coagulation" to "solution."

17. "At all times let us invoke Him, the object of our meditations, in order that our mind may always be absorbed in Him, and our attention concentrated on Him daily" (Nicholas Cabasilas: *Life in Jesus Christ*). What the invocation of the Divine Name is in relation to other prayers, the Eucharist is for the other sacramants: "One receives the Eucharist last, precisely because one can go no further, add nothing to it: for clearly the first term implies the second, and this the last. Now, after the Eucharist there is nothing further towards which one could tend: a stop must be made there, and thought given to the means of keeping, to the end, the good acquired" (ibid.).

18. That is to say "Christ alone is God" — not: "God is Christ" — just as the sun alone is "our sun," that of our planetary system. We need not here return to the question — practically non-existent as it is for the vast majority of ancient and even modern Christians — of knowing where the bounds of the "planetary system" which is Christianity are drawn; this involves the whole problem of the refraction of the celestial in the terrestrial, or more precisely of the concordance between the divine Light and different human receptacles.

19. And because the Absolute has entered into man, into space, into time, the world and history have become as if absolute, whence the

it grafts itself so to speak, not onto the fundamentally theomorphic properties of our nature, but onto the accident — practically speaking decisive for the majority — of our fall; but starting from this point of view — and this is of capital importance — the Christian tradition can give access to gnosis and thus rejoin the perspectives founded on the intellectual theomorphism of the human being, owing to the evident — and dazzling — analogy between Christ and the Intellect, as well as to the idea of deification deriving from it.

To say that "God became man in order that man might become God"[20] means in the final analysis — if we want to pursue this reciprocity to its ultimate foundations — that Reality has entered into nothingness, so that nothingness might become real. If it be objected here that nothingness, being nothing, can play no part, the answer lies in two questions: how is the existence of the very idea of nothingness to be explained? How is it that there is a "nothing" on the level of relativities and in everyday experience? Nothingness certainly has neither being nor existence, but it is nonetheless a kind of metaphysical "direction," something we can conceive and pursue, but never attain; evil is none other than "nothingness manifested" or "the impossible made possible." Evil never lives from its own substance, which is non-existent, but it

danger of an anti-metaphysical conception of the "real," or the temptation of involving God — the Absolute that has become in a sense human or historical — in the "current of forms." This is not unconnected with a theological "personalism" which would seek to substitute the humanized Divine for the Divine-in-Itself, as It reveals Itself to pure Intellect. When we say "absolute" in speaking of the Word or of Being, it is not through failing to recognize that these aspects belong metaphysically to the relative realm, of which they mark the summit *in divinis,* but because, in relation to the cosmos, every aspect of God is absolute.

20. For example, Saint Irenaeus: "Thanks to His boundless love, God made Himself what we are, in order to make us what He is."

corrodes or perverts the good, just as disease could not exist without the body which it tends to destroy; evil, says Saint Thomas, is there to allow the coming of a greater good, and in fact qualities have need of corresponding privations to enable them to be affirmed distinctively and separately.

But in Christianity this reciprocity has first of all a meaning of love, considering its solicitude in regard to efficacy for salvation: the Name of Christ signifies that God loved the world in order that the world might love God; and since God loves the world, man must love his neighbor, thus repeating on the human plane God's love for the world. Likewise, man must "lose his life" because God sacrificed Himself for him;[21] the cross is the instrument and the symbol of this sacrificial meeting, it is as it were the point of intersection between the human and the Divine. Christianity presents itself above all as a volitive reciprocity between Heaven and earth, not as an intellective discernment between Absolute and relative; but this discernment is nonetheless implicit in the reciprocity as such, so that the Christian perspective could not exclude it: the Subject makes itself object in order that the object become Subject, which is the very definition of the mystery of knowledge. Gnosis is based — "organically" and not artificially — on the polyvalent symbolism of the Incarnation and the Redemption, which implies that such a symbiosis is in the nature of things and consequently within the divine intention.

The Name of Christ is "Truth" and "Mercy"; however, this second quality is crystallized in a particular fashion in the Name of the Virgin, so that the two Names appear like

21. In the Eucharistic rite, man eats or drinks God in order to be eaten or drunken by Him; the "elect of the elect" are those who drink and are consumed in a divine wine where there is no longer either "Thee" or "Me."

a polarization of the divine Light. Christ is "Truth and Power" and the Virgin, "Mercy and Purity."[22]

*

* *

Before going further, we must open a parenthesis here: in one of our previous works we said that a Christian can be only either a child of his times or a saint, while a Moslem, or a Jew, can be either an exoterist or an esoterist, and that it is only by virtue of this second quality that he realizes sanctity; in Islam, we said, there is no sanctity outside esoterism, and in Christianity there is no esoterism outside sanctity.[23] To understand this properly, it is necessary to recall that logically and in principle, the exoterism transcended by Christ is the Mosaic Law; now this Law, like every exoterism properly so called — and consequently like the Moslem *sharī'ah* — demands essentially the sincere[24] observance of a body of prescriptions, whereas Christianity aims at replacing the external Law or the "letter" by a personal and qualitative attitude, while becoming dogmatist in its turn.[25]

22. In many icons the Holy Virgin expresses mercy by the inclined and spiral-like movement of her posture, while the severity of her facial expression indicates purity in its aspect of inviolability; other icons express solely this purity, emphasizing the severity of the features by a very upright position; others again express mercy alone, combining the inclination of the body with sweetness of expression.

23. *Spiritual Perspectives and Human Facts*, the chapter "Contours of the Spirit" (Perennial Books, Ltd., 1987).

24. Without this element of sincerity, which results from faith, the observance of these prescriptions would be of no use.

25. It is doubtless this dogmatization or crystallization of an initiatic "wine" which causes Moslems — who like the Jews are guardians of an exoterism de jure — to say that the Christian message *(risālah)* became "corrupted" — a quite exoteric definition, certainly, but instructive from the point of view which interests us here. Let us recall that for the Sufis, Christ brought only a *ḥaqīqah* ("inward" truth), an idea which is indeed proper to Islam as such, since to the saying of Christ: "My kingdom is not of this world," the Prophet in a

This partial and conditional "coagulation" is due, not to unforeseen circumstances — which are anyhow excluded in such a case — but to the original intention of the divine Founder, who sent the Apostles to "teach all nations"; now sanctity brings this de facto exoterism back to its essence, which is de jure esoterism — on the plane of love and in opposition to the outwardness of the Jewish Law[26] — and this is what allowed us to write that there is no Christian "bhaktic" esoterism outside sanctity. But there is yet another dimension to be considered: Christianity includes in addition an esoterism in the absolute sense, and this is,

sense "replies" when he says: "I bring you not only the goods of the other world, I bring you those of this world as well," namely definite rules for individual and social behavior. As we wrote in one of our previous works: "If esoterism does not concern everyone, it is for the reason, analogically speaking, that light penetrates some substances and not others; but on the other hand, if esoterism must manifest itself openly from time to time, as happened in the case of Christ, and, at a lower level of universality, in the case of Al-Hallaj, it is — still by analogy — because the sun illuminates everything without distinction. Thus, if the 'light shineth in darkness' in the principial or universal sense we are concerned with here, this is because in so doing it manifests one of its possibilities, and a possibility, by definition, is something that cannot not be, being an aspect of the absolute necessity of the Divine Principle." *(The Transcendent Unity of Religions,* the chapter "Universality and Particular Nature of the Christian Tradition," p. 135, Quest Books 1993.) This externalizing of an esoterism was for the West the last plank of salvation, the other traditional structures being for it either exhausted or quite inapplicable; but this "anomaly" was at the same time indirectly and "by rebound" — although providentially — the cause of the "offence which needs must come," and this anomaly alone can explain the multitude and extent of the errors in the West, or certain paradoxical features such as the habit of swearing or blaspheming, which is singularly widespread in Christian lands, but unknown in the East. This was what Islam, which seeks to be a normative totality and non-temporal equilibrium, implicitly foresaw.

26. What is in question here is not the Kabbala, which being what *Moysi doctrina velat,* is at least in certain respects like "Christianity before its time."

precisely, gnosis or "theosophy."[27] It will then not only be sanctity with a volitive and emotional basis, but also sapiential doctrine and a fortiori the sanctity which refers to it, which we shall qualify as "esoterism," if we have a reason for using this term which is in itself irreproachable; and let us recall in this context the correlation between the "Peace" of Christ and pure contemplation.[28] Gnosis, while in a certain way going beyond faith and love — since knowledge finally goes beyond thought and will — represents in another respect their quasi-divine mode.

*

* *

In Islam, the implicit doctrine of the Name of God is Unity; Unity must be understood to mean that God is the Absolute and that there is but one Absolute; that it is this global aspect of evidentness or of absoluteness which "unifies," that is to say transmutes and delivers. He who says *Allāh* says "there is no Truth or Absolute but the one Truth, the one Absolute" (to paraphrase the *Shahādah: Lā ilāha illā 'Llāh),* or in Vedantic terms: "The world is false, *Brahma* is real"; or again: "Nothing is evident, if not the Absolute." And this amounts to saying that Islam takes its starting point not in our fallen, passional nature, but in the theomorphic, inalterable character of our humanity, that is, in what distinguishes us from animals, namely objective and in principle limitless intelligence. Now the normal content of the intelligence — that for which it is made — is the Absolute-Infinite; in a word, man is intelligence at once integral and transcendent,

27. Genuine "theosophy" is to theology what gnosis is to faith, although from another point of view gnosis and theosophy cannot be situated outside faith and theology respectively.

28. We have treated all these questions in *Spiritual Perspectives and Human Facts,* the chapter "Knowledge and Love," (Perennial Books, Ltd., 1987).

horizontal and vertical, and the essential content of this intelligence is at the same time our Deliverance; man is delivered by consciousness of the Absolute, his salvation is the remembrance of God.

Consequently, the simple fact that we are men obliges us to "become One"; we have no choice, for we cannot demand of destiny to make birds or flowers of us; we are condemned to the Infinite. A receptacle necessitates a content: if there were no water, nor milk, nor wine, then jugs and waterskins would have no right to exist; likewise for our spirit, which is made in order that it may know the Evidence[29] which delivers. The human state commits to a "knowing," and this knowing commits to a "being": to believe sincerely what the Name *Allāh* implies — namely that *lā ilāha illā 'Llāh* — is by the same token to assume the consequences of this conviction and to profess, by practicing it, Unity on all planes, social as well as spiritual; that which is normative — namely a factor of equilibrium or of union[30] — on whatever plane, reveals itself by that very fact as a manifestation of Unity, or as a participation in It. There is no *īmān* (unitary faith) without *islām* (submission to the Law), and there is neither one nor the other without *iḥsān* (spiritual virtue), that is to say without profound understanding or realization; he who accepts the One has already given himself *(aslama)*

29. The French word *"évidence"* is often translated as "evidence" in this and related passages; but it is necessary to keep in mind that in such contexts the word includes the meaning of "evidentness" (or self-evidence). (Translator's note)

30. Equilibrium as regards the collectivity and union as regards the individual; but there is no radical division here, the individual also having need of equilibrium and the collectivity participating in its way, by religion, in union. To say that the collectivity is something other than the individual does not mean that this involves a radical incompatibility, or that these two poles of the human condition do not influence one another. Morals are the ascesis of the collectivity, just as ascesis constitutes the morals of the individual.

to Him, unless he is to lose himself in a mortal[31] hypocrisy *(nifāq)*. To admit the existence of some relativity may obligate one to nothing or may obligate one to a merely relative position; to admit the Absolute obligates a man totally.

But the Name *Allāh*, besides its aspect of Truth or of Evidence, also comprises the aspect of Mercy, and it is then equivalent to the formula of consecration: "In the Name of God (the Unique), the infinitely Good or Blessed (in Himself) and the infinitely Merciful (as regards the world)" *(bismi 'Llāhi 'r-Raḥmāni 'r-Raḥīm)*.[32] This Mercy God manifests by his Revelations as also by the symbols and gifts of nature, the word "sign" *(ayah)* referring to both categories, the one supernatural and the other natural; the meaning of the formula of consecration is thus very close to that of the second testimony of faith: "Muhammad is the Messenger of God."[33] The testimony that God is One enunciates the absorption of the human or the earthly by "Truth," while the testimony that Muhammad — and with him all the Revealers[34] — is the Messenger of the One God, marks the

31. The Mosaic revelation — Judaism properly so called — puts all its emphasis on the element *islām*, or more exactly on the formal, or formalist, aspect of this element, so that the quality giving salvation is here that of being an "Israelite," a man's attachment to a divine framework, and not a priori a character pre-existing in human nature.

32. In this formula, the *Basmalah*, the first term — "in the Name of God" — indicates the divine Causality, while the first of the two divine Names which follow indicates the "divine Substance" — or the "underlying Beatitude" — of the cosmos, and the second the divine Mercy insofar as it enters into the cosmos by discontinuous influences and feeds it "successively" with its gifts and its graces.

33. The difference between the *Basmalah* and the second *Shahādah* lies in the fact that the latter proceeds "from below upward" and the former "from above downward": the *Basmalah* is the formula of divine manifestation, creation, revelation, while the second *Shahādah* on the contrary indicates ascent, realization, the path.

34. According to Saint Thomas, faith in the existence (the reality) of God and faith in Providence are indispensable to salvation: "In the

effusion of virtues and graces in the world or in the soul, and thus compensates the negative aspect that the first testimony has in relation to the cosmos. If the first testimony bears witness that "the world is false, *Brahma* is true," the second does not let us forget that "all is *Ātmā.*"[35]

The Koran indicates the conditions — and outlines the framework — of the orison of the "isolated" *(mufrad)* or "supreme" *(a'zham)* Name, in enjoining the invocation of *Allāh* "with humility and in secret," and also "through fear and through desire" (VII, 55 and 56); it says moreover: "Be steadfast and remember God often" (VIII, 45), without neglecting the aspect of quietude: "Is is not through remembrance of God that hearts repose in security?" (XIII, 28). From this derives the following doctrine: we must fear God — and in fact it is Him alone that we fear, without knowing it — that is to say we must not "take the name of the Lord in vain" (Exod. 20:7), namely with an impure intention aimed at the approval of men or at glory, or even at magic; we must desire God — and in fact it is Him alone that we desire, without knowing it[36] — that is to say we must pronounce His Name "with all our mind, with all our soul and all our strength" (Deut. 6:5);[37] as to humility, it is indispensable, for it is the consciousness of our nothingness, which is determined by consciousness of the All-Reality; and as for secrecy, the divine Name demands it, for this Name has no feature of collective devotion, its realm not

existence of God are contained all things that we believe to exist (to be real) eternally in God; and in faith in Providence are included all the dispensations of God in time concerned with the salvation of men" *(Summa Theologica* II, II, 1, 7).

35. On the Christian side and from the point of view of gnosis, the assertion that Christ alone is God combines in its way the two testimonies of Islam, or rather the two corresponding metaphysical angles of vision.

36. The love of God implies love of the neighbor, just as the fear of God implies flight from sin, that is fear of its consequences.

37. This is equivalent, despite the diversity of possible applications, to the Hindu triad *jnāna, bhakti* and *karma*.

being the communal Law. But secrecy has also a quite inward sense and then refers to the "heart" as the symbolical seat of the Self; finally, the resoluteness and frequency of "remembering" conquer space and time, the world and life; and as for the "repose of hearts," it is in God alone that we find Peace.

The Name *Allāh* contains all these meanings. *Allāh* who is the Unique, is thereby the great Peace: being pure Reality, there is in Him no disequilibrium, no narrowness. His Name is the Peace which silences all the sounds of the world, be they around us or within us, in accordance with this verse: "Say: *Allāh!* then leave them to their vain talk" (Koran, VI, 91).[38] Thus over the things of this world or of our soul the Name throws as it were an immense blanket of snow extinguishing all, and uniting all in one same purity and one same overflowing and eternal silence.

*

* *

The Hindu who invokes Shri Rama abandons his own existence for that of his Lord: it is as if he were asleep and Rama were watching and acting for him; he sleeps in Shri Rama, in the divine form of Him who is invoked, who takes on all the burdens of the life of the devotee and in the end brings him back into this divine and immutable form itself. The doctrine of Rama is contained in the *Rāmayāna:* the myth retraces the destiny of the soul (Sita) ravished by passion and ignorance (Ravana) and exiled in matter, at the confines of the cosmos (Lanka). Every soul devoted to Shri Rama is identified with Sita, the heroine carried off and

38. "The most noble of words is the utterance of *Allāh,*" says the Prophet, which means that this Name contains all words, and makes all words superfluous. "Every creature — sings Mahmud Shabistari — has its existence from the Unique Name, from which it comes and to which it returns with endless praises." "God has cursed everything on earth, save the remembrance [the invocation] of God" (*Ḥadīth*).

then delivered.[39] Radha, the eternal spouse of Krishna, lends herself to the same symbolism; and he who says Krishna sets forth the wisdom hidden in the *Mahābhārata* and expounded in the *Bhagavad Gītā,* which is its synthesis and its flower.

*

*   *

The invocation of the Buddha Amitabha — the Logos inasmuch as it transmigrates accumulating "merits" and, being the Logos, returns "with full right" to its original and nirvanic plenitude — this invocation is founded on a doctrine of redemption, that of the "original Vow." Amitabha — the Japanese Amida — is the Light and the Life of the Buddha Shakyamuni; through invoking Amitabha the devotee enters into a golden halo of Mercy, he finds security in the blessed light of that Name; he withdraws into it with perfect surrender and also with perfect gratitude.[40] The whole of Amidism is contained in these words: purity, invocation, faith: abstaining from evil, invoking the Name, having trust.[41] Amida is Light and Life;[42] His Name carries the

39. The ordeal of Sita — Rama doubting her fidelity — refers to the discontinuity between the "I" and the "Self," to the hiatus in the incommensurable dialogue between the soul and the Lord; the repudiation of Sita and her return to her mother, the Earth, signifies that the ego as such remains always the ego. But the eternal Sita is none other than Lakshmi, spouse of Rama-Vishnu, and she it is who *in divinis* is the prototype of the soul.

40. In Amidism, gratitude is what we could call the "moral stimulus."

41. This triad belongs to every path founded on the power of divine Names. Abstention from evil is the passive condition; faith or trust the active condition.

42. It is the aspect Amitayus (issued from the forehead of Amitabha) which relates more particularly to "infinite Life." When the historical Buddha speaks of "previous Buddhas," it is as if He spoke of Himself, in the sense that they incarnate the aspects of His nature and that they are of His essence, or of the essence of the unique and universal Buddha, the Adi-Buddha, who is the "celestial body" — *the Dharma-Kāya* — of all

faithful towards the "Western Paradise" *(Sukhāvatī):* the devotee follows the solar Name through to its consummation, "to the West"[43] — he follows it right into the hereafter, leaving the world behind him, in the night — he follows this sun which, having traversed the "round of Existence," is "thus gone" *(tathāgāta),* or which is "gone, gone not to return, gone to the other shore" *(gāte, pāragāte, pārasamgāte).*

*
* *

Orison implies an inner alternative, a choice between an imperfection arising from our nature, and the remembrance of God, which is perfection by reason of its prime mover as well as of its object. If this alternative is above all an inner one — otherwise we would have no right to any

Buddhas. In Amidism, it is Amitabha who is identified with the universal Buddha; from another point of view, as we have just said, the "mystical" Buddhas personify aspects of Shakyamuni, in the sense that Amitabha, Vairochana, Akshobya, Ratnasambhava and Amoghasiddhi — the five *'Dhyāni Buddhas"* — each relate to one of the great moments of the life of the historical Buddha, but also a priori to one of the great cosmic cycles, not forgetting the cosmic "regions" and the aspects or functions of the universal Intellect, these latter being represented, among other things, by mental faculties and the former by the directions of space. Outside the specifically Amidist perspective, it is Vairochana — as Mahavairochana (Dainichi in Japanese) — who is identified with Adi-Buddha and who, remaining "at the center," produces by irradiation the four other *'Dhyāni Buddhas."* In Hindu terms, Adi-Buddha or Vairochana — and Amitabha or Shakyamuni insofar as they are identified with them — will be *Chit* (the enlightening, but not the creating Purusha) and its comsic reflection Buddhi or Sarasvati.

43. As for the East, it indicates the Paradise of the Buddha Akshobya (Ashuku in Japanese), conqueror of the demon (Mara); the East is attributed also — outside the sphere of the five *'Dhyāni Buddhas"* — to the Buddha Bhaishajyaguru (Yakushi), who drives away maladies like the rising sun drives away darkness, and whose mercy more particularly concerns this terrestrial world, whereas that of Amitabha is manifested in the other world.

outward action — it is because prayer can be superimposed on any legitimate action; likewise, if the alternative is relative and not absolute — otherwise we would have no right to any thought outside prayer — it is because orison, if it cannot be superimposed on every beautiful or useful thought, can at least continue to vibrate during the course of such a thought; and then mental articulation, although in practice excluding prayer — to the extent that the mind cannot do two things at once — nevertheless does not interrupt the "remembrance" in the eyes of God. In other words, just as prayer cannot be superimposed on a base or illicit action, so the fragrance of prayer cannot subsist during a thought opposed to the virtues; further, it is obvious that the vibration of prayer in the absence of its articulation — when the mind is engaged elsewhere — presupposes a habit of prayer in the subject, for there is no scent without a flower; it presupposes also the intention to persevere in prayer and to intensify it; it is thus that the "past" and the "future," the acquired and the intended, participate in the unarticulated continuity of prayer.

Life is not, as children and worldly people believe, a kind of space filled with possibilities offering themselves to our good pleasure; it is a road which becomes more and more narrow, from the present moment to death. At the end of this road there is death and the encounter with God, then eternity; now, all these realities are already present in prayer, in the timeless actuality of the divine Presence.

What matters, for man, is not the diversity of the events he may experience as they stretch out along the magic thread we call duration, but perseverance in the remembrance which takes us outside time and raises us above our hopes and our fears. This remembrance already dwells in eternity; in it the succession of actions is only illusory, prayer being one; prayer is thereby already a death, a meeting with God, an eternity of bliss.

What is the world if not a flow of forms, and what is life if not a cup which seemingly is emptied between one night and another? And what is prayer, if not the sole stable point — a point of peace and light — in this dream universe, and the strait gate leading to all that the world and life have sought in vain? In the life of a man, these four certitudes are all: the present moment, death, the encounter with God, eternity. Death is an exit, a world which closes down; the meeting with God is like an opening towards a fulgurating and immutable infinitude; eternity is a fullness of being in pure light; and the present moment is, in our duration, an almost ungraspable "place" where we are already eternal — a drop of eternity amid the ceaseless shiftings of forms and melodies. Prayer gives to the terrestrial instant its full weight of eternity and its divine value; it is the sacred ship bearing its load, through life and death, towards the further shore, towards the silence of light — but at bottom it is not prayer which traverses time as it repeats itself, it is time which, so to speak, halts before the already celestial unicity of prayer.

The Stations of Wisdom

Human nature comprises three planes: the plane of the will, the plane of love and the plane of knowledge; each is polarized into two complementary modes, which appear, respectively, as renunciation and act, peace and fervor, discernment and union.

The will is divided in a certain sense into an affirmative mode and a negative mode, for it can only accomplish or abstain: it must either do "good" or avoid "evil." In spiritual life, the negative attitude comes in principle before the positive or affirmative act, because the will is a priori entrenched in its state — natural since the fall — of passional and blind affirmation; every spritual path must start with a "conversion," an apparently negative turning round of the will, an indirect movement towards God in the form of an inner separation from the false plenitude of the world. This withdrawal corresponds to the station of renunciation or detachment, of sobriety, of fear of God: what has to be overcome is desire, passional attachment, idolatry of ephemeral things; the error of passion is proven by its connection with impurtiy, corruption, suffering and death.[1] The divine prototype of the virtue of detachment is

1. Gnosis objectifies sin — error carried into action — by referring it back to its impersonal causes, but subjectifies the definition of sin by making the quality of action depend on personal intention. The moral perspective, on the contrary, subjectifies the act by identifying it as it were

Purity, Impassibility, Immortality; this quality, whether we envisage it *in divinis* or in ourselves, or around us, is like crystal, or snow, or the cold serenity of high mountains; in the soul the virtue of detachment is a spiritual anticipation of death and thereby a victory over it. It is fixation in instantaneity, in spiritual motionlesness, in the fear of God.

The will, as we have said, must both deny and affirm: if it must deny by reason of the falsity of its habitual objects, which are impermanent, it must on the other hand affirm by reason of its positive character, which is freedom of choice. Since the spiritual act must assert itself with force against the lures of the world or of the soul which seek to engross and corrupt the will, it involves the combative virtues: decision, vigilance, perseverance; and it is in turn conditioned by them, not in its unique actuality, but in its relationship with duration, which demands repetition, rhythm, the transmutation of time into instantaneity; the spiritual act is, on its own plane, a participation in Omnipotence, in the divine Liberty, in the pure and eternal Act. What has to be actively conquered is natural and habitual passivity towards the world and towards the images and impulsions of the soul; spiritual laziness, inattention, dreaming, all have to be overcome; what gives victory is the divine Presence which is "incarnate" as it were in the sacred act — prayer in all its forms — and thus regenerates the individual substance. The symbols of this spiritual station — that of combat, victory, pure act — are lightning and the sword; it is, *in divinis*, fulgurating and invincible Perfection, and in man, holy anger or holy warfare, but above all the inward act as affirmation of the Self.

*

* *

with the agent, but objectifies the definition of sin by making the quality of the act depend on its form, and so on an external standard.

On the plane of love, of the affective life of the soul, we can distinguish an active mode and a passive mode, as in everything that lives. Passive virtue is made of contemplative contentment, hence also of patience; it is the calm of that which rests in itself, in its own virtue; it is generous relaxation, harmony; it is repose in pure Being, equilibrium of all possibilities. This attitude loosens the knots of the soul, it removes agitation, dissipation, and the contraction which is the static counterpart of agitation; there is in it neither curiosity nor disquiet. The quality of calm derives from the divine Peace, which is made of Beatitude, of infinite Beauty; beauty everywhere and always has at its root an aspect of calm, of existential repose,[2] of equilibrium of possibilities; this is to say that it has an aspect of limitlessness and of happiness. The essence of the soul is beatitude; what makes us strangers to ourselves is dissipation, which casts us into destitution and ugliness, into a state of sterile dilapidation similar to shaking palsy, a disordered movement which has become a state, whereas normally it is the static which is at the basis of the dynamic and not the converse. Beauty bears within itself every element of happiness, whence its character of peace, plenitude, satisfaction; now beauty is in our very being, we live by its substance. It is the calm, simple and generous perfection of the pool which mirrors the depth of the sky with all its serenity; it is the beauty of the water lily, of the lotus opening to the light of the sun.[3] It is repose in the center, resignation to Provi-

2. Let us recall here that virtue for the *Philokalia*, is "the natural state of the soul," and this enables us also to grasp what the Asiatic traditions mean when they speak of "going beyond the virtues": a virtue is a limit insofar as it is an expression of ourselves, and it is transcended — or realized to the full, which amounts to the same thing — when it no longer belongs to us in any way as our own.

3. It will be remembered here that Buddhist iconography represents the Buddha seated on a lotus, and that the Buddha is called "Jewel in the lotus" (*mani padmē*). The Buddhas bring salvation not only by their teaching, but also by their superhuman beauty.

dence, quietude in God. We can distinguish in this station a gentle aspect and a stern aspect, namely the happy quietude founded on the certainty that all we love is to be found infinitely in God, and the ascetic contentment founded on the idea that God suffices us.

But beside this repose in our initial equilibrium or in our existential perfection, there is a positive tendency that is converse, a "going out of oneself" in active mode; this is fervor, confident and charitable faith; it is the melting of the heart in the divine warmth, its opening to Mercy, to essential Life, to infinite Love. Man, in his fallen state, is closed to the Mercy which seeks to save him; this is hardness of heart, indifference towards God and the neighbor, egoism, greed, mortal triviality; such triviality is as it were the inverse counterpart of hardness, it is the fragmenting of the soul among sterile facts, among their insignificant and empty multiplicity, their desiccating drab monotony; it is the chop and change of "ordinary life" where ugliness and boredom pose as "reality." In this state, the soul is both hard like stone and pulverized like sand, it lives among the dead husks of things and not in the Essence which is Life and Love; it is at once hardness and dissolution. Wholly different from this dissolution is the spiritual liquefaction of the ego; this is fervor, intense unification of the movements of the soul in an upsurge of faith in the divine Mercy: it is also the warm, gentle quality of spring, or that of fire melting ice and restoring life to frozen limbs. Charitable acceptance of the neighbor is a necessary manifestation of this alchemical liquefaction of the heart; it is as it were the criterion of that tendency — or state — of the intelligence and the will which we can call "love of God." This is so firstly because egoism, which is a form of petrifaction, is compensated and overcome by every "going outside" ourselves, and secondly because God appears in our neighbor; in other words, one must love God not only in losing oneself, but also in recognizing Him in others. This spiritual quality is like fire, which burns and liquefies, or like blood, which gives life to bodies from within; it is also like love, or wine, which produce intoxication and seem to bring everything back to the essences, or like the red rose, whose color burns and whose perfume is inebriating. Besides its active aspect founded on the conviction that God surely responds to our fervor,[4] this station includes a passive aspect, founded on the melting of the heart in the divine Warmth; there is in this second attitude as it were a noble sadness, something related to the gift of tears and the path of mystical love; it like nostalgia for the Beauty of the Loved One. Joy and melancholy meet in fervor, as beatitude and sobriety — or hope and resignation — meet in peace.

*
* *

The plane of knowledge, which by definition goes beyond the realm of the ego as such, comprises a separative mode and a unitive mode, as the very nature of gnosis requires: or, as could also be said, an objective mode and a subjective mode, in the deepest sense of these terms. Knowledge in fact operates either by discernment or by identification: either it is "perceiving" or "conceiving," or else it is "being." Discriminative knowledge separates the unreal from the Real; the mind must be conscious of the nothingness of the ego and of the world; it must surmount the congenital confusion which attributes to the unreal the quality of the Real; it must empty the ego, and empty itself of the ego, because the one, unique Reality can be known only in the void. To see the oneness of the Real is to see at the same time our own nothingness; however, to see our nothingness is not to see Reality in a direct and total manner; unitive knowledge alone can realize wholeness. Discriminative knowledge is like the night when the moon is

4. "Knock, and it shall be opened unto you," says the Gospel. Fervor is in fact affirmed by tirelessly repeated appeals, as several passages of the New Testament bear witness.

shining: we easily distinguish the moon from the night, but though the light of the moon is indeed that of the sun, we are not in broad daylight. In this perspective of metaphysical discrimination the subject is false, the Object alone is true; the subject is individuation, illusion, limitation; the Object — that is to say that which is "outside us" — is the Principle, the Absolute.

But if the spirit can "know Reality," it can also, in principle if not in fact, "realize the Knower"; in this realization — unitive knowledge — the Subject is true and the object is false; the Subject is the infinite Self, and the object is that which veils It, namely, limited or objectified consciousness. In this ultimate knowledge, there is no longer discernment, there is but pure Light;[5] it is identity, not confrontation. The ego is otherness; it is separative illusion, the error of believing that I am identified with the empirical "I" composed of outward and inward experiences, mental images and volitions; it is introducing a division into Reality. The truth is "to become That which we are," and so to identify ourselves with our own Essence. But our thought is incapable of going ontologically beyond objectification and fundamental dualism, for it is by definition separative in its very substance; in relation to Reality it is like the color white in relation to light: white is distinct from black, but is

5. However, once this viewpoint of unitive knowledge is stated in a doctrinal, and so mental form, it has need in its turn of discernment because neither the discursive mind, nor the world in which it operates are in the state of union. This is why the Vedanta discerns between the pure Subject and objectification or illusion; its central truth is not, however, this discernment, but the Self and identity with the Self. Let us recall once more that pure metaphysics is essentially symbolist and descriptive, not literal and conjectural: in fact, to describe what one sees is quite a different thing from making constructions of what one does not see. Or again: the depth of a statement and its fecundity in no way depend on its formal complexity; the value of an expression lies in the depth of the truth it actualizes for those to whom it is by its very nature addressed.

invisible without light and could not illuminate anything. Now, if our "being" must become "knowing" — and this is the point of view of discernment — our "knowing" must become "being"; if, on the one hand, instead of "existing" it is necessary to "discern," then it is necessary, on the other hand, to "be" instead of to "think"; for thought indicates a direction, but does not attain the goal; it does not embrace our entire being, still less total Reality.

The two stations or degrees of knowledge could be respectively characterized by the following formulas: "To know only That which is: God"; "To be only That which knows: the Self." Or again: "Extinction of the subject by virtue of the Unicity of the Object, which is without associate"; "Extinction of objects by virtue of the Unity of the Subject, which is without scission." If we represent Truth — or Reality — by a circle, we could say that the first point of view eliminates an error comparable to the duplication of the unique circle, while the second point of view eliminates an error comparable to the scission of this same figure. The first error, as we have seen, adds to the Reality of God that of the world, including the ego, while the second error cuts off the knowing "I" — the intellectual and sensory subject — from its divine Source; the world and the ego are indeed separated from God when considered as contents, whether subjective or objective, but they are "identified" with Him — the world with Being and the ego with the Self — in the respective relationships of Existence and Intelligence.[6] God — in the total sense which transcends "Person" and "Being" — is "pure Object" and

---

6. The relationship "Existence" includes symbolism, which is its intellectual aspect and connects the contents to the Prototypes; symbolism is in a way the intelligence of things. Conversely, the relationship "Intelligence" has an existential aspect: what symbolism is for things, the "person" is for consciousness; symbols are things "qualified" by Intelligence, and the person is consciousness "fixed" or "coagulated" by Existence.

"unique"; the Self is the "pure Subject," the one and indivisible "Witness"; God is the Self.

There is then, in these two metaphysical perspectives, and as between one and the other, an inversion of the subject and the complement; the first perspective is "to know Being," the exclusive Reality; the second is "to be Knowledge," undifferentiated Consciousness. It is necessary to know That which alone is, and to be That which alone knows. In the first of these stations, the subject is "void," since it is determined by the Object, which is the unique Reality; it is reduced to its content[7] or rather it is excluded or annihilated by objective Reality; in the second station, the subject is "identified" with its Essence, that is to say it is absorbed and integrated by the infinite Consciousness, in relation to which the relative subject is an "objectification," like the entire cosmos.

I am, therefore I am all, principially and virtually; my being as such is all the Being there is. Likewise: I know, therefore I know all; my knowledge as such is all the Knowledge there is. However: my knowledge, insofar as it is individual, must become being; and likewise: my being, insofar as it is individual, must become knowledge, consciousness, ipseity.[8]

*

* *

The plane of the will, which comprises the stations of renunciation and of act, and the plane of love, which comprises the stations of contentment and of fervor, belong either to exoterism or to esoterism, according to the levels of understanding and of application; the plane of love is,

7. "The soul is all that it knows," says Aristotle.

8. For the gnostic — always in the etymological and not the sectarian sense of the term — or for the *jnani*, there can be no question of "egoism," since the ego is not "himself." The "I" is for him the "other," objectification, the vital tangible center of the world.

however, by its "liquid" nature, nearer to esoterism than is the plane of the will. As for the plane of knowledge, it belongs exclusively to esoterism; it includes, as we have seen, doctrinal understanding on the one hand, and unitive wisdom on the other. All these stations concern on the one hand God, the Metacosm, and on the other, the soul, the microcosm; but they are thereby also keys for the "alchemical" comprehension of the world, the macrocosm. From another angle, if these positions by the very fact that they are contemplative presuppose the fundamental virtues, still more do they imply these virtues and sublimate them.

The perspective of metaphysical discernment, of the unique and exclusive Reality, is like a synthesis, but on the plane of the intellect and in transcendent mode, of the two perspectives of the will, that of detachment and that of action; in an analogous way, the perspective of identity or of the Self, is like a synthesis, but on the plane of unitive knowledge and beyond the human level, of the perspectives of peace and of fervor. The viewpoint of fervor or of life is harmoniously opposable to that of detachment or of death, just as the viewpoint of contentment or of peace is opposable without antinomy to that of action or of combat.

These fundamental positions of wisdom can be combined in different ways, and each can serve as a point of departure. It will have been noticed that Christian mysticism is closely akin to the perspective of renunciation and purity, as also to that of love and mercy; Christianity thus compensates its aspect of renunciation by the passion of love. Buddhism also takes renunciation as its starting point, but is akin rather to the perspective of peace and beatitude; it compensates its renunciation with the peace of Nirvana. As for Islam, it is like a combination between the perspective of combat and that of peace; it compensates its combative aspect by its aspect of equilibrium, resignation, generosity. The Vedanta — and all gnosis — is founded on discernment between the Real and the unreal, and compensates the specifically intellectual — and non-volitive — content of this perspective by the "existential" (or rather the supra-existential) concretization which is identification with the Self. All these indications are no doubt very schematic, but there are things which cannot be said without some risk, and which one must nonetheless risk saying. However that may be, it is important not to lose sight of the fact that each tradition includes in one way or another, and of necessity, all these six stations of wisdom, even if those belonging to gnosis must sometimes withdraw behind veils of esoteric symbolism.

Independently of these considerations, we would like also to suggest the following relationships: the world is division, movement, becoming, disquiet, and so we too are divided, restless, changeable, anxious. It is to this cosmic spectacle that the evidentness of Unity responds (Islam), unity of God, of the soul, of society, of metaphysical Reality;[9] likewise, the evidentness of "God made man" (Christianity) answers to the spectacle of sinful nature, of human impotence, of the downfall of our will; or again the evidentness of renunciation and of extinction (Buddhism) answers to the spectacle of universal suffering and instability.[10]

*
* *

Some people see a kind of incompatibility between metaphysics — which they confuse with the more or less logical constructions of the discursive mind — and the love of God, of which they seem to see only the most human side. Let us

9. The emphasis is placed on Unity, because Unity is evident; to say Unity is to say self-evidence, truth, reality, absoluteness, and then grounds for existence and for living.

10. *Nirvāna* is the "motionless center" of the "cosmic wheel"; the Buddha is the manifestation of the "Void," in the sense that the Reality of Nirvana appears as void in relation to the world; Buddhahood (*bodhi*, "illumination"), is to realize that the wheel is none other than the "Void," in the negative as in the transcendent sense of the term.

recall here that the love of God is something universal: the term "love" designates not only a path depending on will and feeling, but also — and this is its broadest meaning — every path insofar as it attaches us to the Divine; "love" is everything which makes us prefer God to the world and contemplation to earthly activity, wherever this alternative has a meaning. The best love will be, not that which most resembles what the word "love" can evoke in us a priori, but that which will attach us most steadfastly or most profoundly to Reality; to love God is to keep oneself near to Him, in the midst of the world and beyond the world; God wants our souls, whatever may be our attitudes or our methods.

And likewise: "God is Love," not only towards creation and because He loves the world, but also in Himself and because He is profoundly steeped in His own infinitude; in the first sense, God is Love because He "wills" the world and therefore is merciful, and the the second sense, He is Love because He wills Himself, or because He wills nothing outside the Self.

All great spiritual experiences agree in this: there is no common measure between the means put into operation and the result. "With men this is impossible, but with God all things are possible," says the Gospel. In fact, what separates man from divine Reality is but a thin partition: God is infinitely close to man, but man is infinitely far from God. This partition, for man, is a mountain; man stands in front of a mountain which he must remove with his own hands. He digs away the earth, but in vain, the mountain remains; man however goes on digging, in the name of God. And the mountain vanishes. It was never there.

INDEX

BY THE SAME AUTHOR

The Transcendent Unity of Religions, *1953*
Revised Edition, *1974, 1984, The Theosophical Publishing House, 1993*

Spiritual Perspectives and Human Facts, *1954, 1969*
New translation, *Perennial Books, 1987*

Gnosis: Divine Wisdom, *1959, 1978, Perennial Books, 1990*

Stations of Wisdom, *1961, 1980*
New translation, *World Wisdom Books, 1995*

Understanding Islam, *1963, 1965, 1972, 1976, 1979, 1981, 1986, 1989*
New translation, *World Wisdom Books, 1994*

Light on the Ancient Worlds, *1966, World Wisdom Books, 1984*

In the Tracks of Buddhism, *1968, 1989*
New translation, Treasures of Buddhism, *World Wisdom Books, 1993*

Logic and Transcendence, *1975, Perennial Books, 1984*

Esoterism as Principle and as Way, *Perennial Books, 1981, 1990*

Castes and Races, *Perennial Books, 1959, 1982*

Sufism: Veil and Quintessence, *World Wisdom Books, 1981*

From the Divine to the Human, *World Wisdom Books, 1982*

Christianity/Islam, *World Wisdom Books, 1985*

The Essential Writings of Frithjof Schuon (S. H. Nasr, Ed.)
1986, Element 1991

Survey of Metaphysics & Esoterism, *World Wisdom Books, 1986*

In the Face of the Absolute, *World Wisdom Books, 1989, 1994*

The Feathered Sun: Plains Indians in Art & Philosophy,
World Wisdom Books, 1990

To Have a Center, *World Wisdom Books, 1990*

Roots of the Human Condition, *World Wisdom Books, 1991*

Images of Primordial & Mystic Beauty: Paintings by Frithjof Schuon,
Abodes, 1992

Echoes of Perennial Wisdom, *World Wisdom Books, 1992*

The Play of Masks, *World Wisdom Books, 1992*

The Transfiguration of Man, *World Wisdom Books, in preparation*

Road to the Heart, *World Wisdom Books, in preparation*